DOCTOR, PLEASE CLOSE THE DOOR!

A book on Living Wills,
Powers of Attorney, terminal care,
and the right to die with dignity

by

Kenneth A. Bartholomew, M.D.

dp
Distinctive Publishing Corp.

Doctor, Please Close the Door! A book on Living Wills,
Powers of Attorney, terminal care, and the right to die with dignity
by Kenneth A. Bartholomew, M.D.
Copyright 1994 by Kenneth A. Bartholomew, M.D.

Published by Distinctive Publishing Corp.
P. O. Box 17868
Plantation, Florida 33318-7868
Printed in the United States of America

ISBN: 0-942963-45-8
Library of Congress No.: 93-39045
Price: $9.95

Library of Congress Cataloging-in-Publication Data

Bartholomew, Kenneth A., 1949-
    Doctor, please close the door! : a book on living wills, powers
of attorney, terminal care, and the right to die with dignity / by
Kenneth A. Bartholomew.
        p. cm.
    ISBN 0-942963-45-8 (paper) : $9.95
        1. Right to die. 2. Terminal care—Moral and ethical
    aspects. 3. Terminally ill—Case studies. 4. Power of
    attorney. I. Title.
R726.B32 1994
174'.24—dc20   93-39045
                                                          CIP

TABLE OF CONTENTS

INTRODUCTION

THE IDEAS, OPINIONS and conclusions portrayed in this book are the result of eleven years of premedical and medical training and sixteen years of medical practice. For fourteen years I have been the medical director of a fifty-four bed, skilled nursing home, as well as being the Chief of Staff of a community hospital for twelve years. I have been the decision maker for hundreds of terminally ill patients.

I would like to take you for a stroll through our nursing home to meet some of the people there. Most of it will not be nice. For those who have never been involved with terminal or elderly care, it may be somewhat uncomfortable, but I hope it will be educational. Although I have altered their names for reasons of confidentiality, each one of the people you are about to meet are real, and their conditions are described as accurately as humanly possible.

I am sure to be criticized by some for what I have to say, but I can only give the facts as I see them—along with my own beliefs and convictions—thereby trying to educate those to whom this is new ground. By doing so, I hope to spur you into the action of taking charge of your terminal care decisions before it is too late and someone else takes charge for you, making decisions you would probably never make for yourself.

1

A QUIET WALK
DOWN THE HALL

LET US BEGIN by taking a quiet walk down
the hall of our nursing home and meeting a few
of the residents there. Not all of our residents are
as ill as the ones you will meet; in fact, many of
them live very happy, comfortable lives playing
cards and bingo, reading books, and watching
television. They get together for social events
every afternoon and simply live in the home
because their age and/or infirmities make it
impossible for them to care for themselves at
home. These are not the people this book is
about. However, most of them will deteriorate
further, unless they are fortunate and are able to
pass quietly from this world.

● ● ●

Fred is an 87-year-old man who moved
into the nursing home when he became too weak
to care for himself. His wife was suffering from
severe senile dementia and could no longer cook
or clean for him and, since he was wheelchair
bound, he could care for neither her nor himself.

Fred's major problem when he entered the nursing home was that of severe, peripheral vascular disease and severe weakness of the legs. He could barely walk, and short walks of 25 to 50 feet completely tired him out.

Peripheral vascular disease is the slow, but deadly, clogging of the arteries from cholesterol plaque that eventually closes off the artery. The tissue that the artery serves with oxygen and nutrients weakens and eventually shrivels and dies. At first Fred was able to function in his wheelchair. The nurses would take him for short walks four times a day to try to preserve some leg function, but he did not like doing this because it was too hard a task to perform and because it became more and more painful. Eventually, as the disease process worsened, he began spending all of his time in his wheelchair or his bed. Of course, the same process that was attacking his legs began attacking his heart and his brain. Fred's memory began to fail, and within two years he was completely bed-bound. His decision-making capacity dwindled rapidly after that.

At about this time his right fourth toe began turning black from dry gangrene because of the absence of blood flow to the tip of the toe. We amputated that toe to try to prevent infection from spreading to the foot, only to find within about a month that three other toes were beginning to turn black and dry on the tips. This eventually spread to all of his toes, and the gangrene slowly inched its way toward the foot. Prior to this, his feet had become very painful. When he was still trying to walk, each step shot electric needles of pain through his feet and up through his legs. Even after he could no longer walk, the pain continued to advance. He began having constant, severe pain in the feet even when lying perfectly still in bed. By this time a typical day in Fred's life was lying in bed, being fed meals because he could no longer feed himself, and receiving pain medications to try to keep him comfortable. The constant use of pain medications further hampered his mental capacity because of narcotic sedation, a necessary evil to keep him comfortable.

In spite of higher and higher doses of narcotics, Fred now lies in bed in constant pain, drooling on his pillow and telling me he wishes he could die. His family wants him to be comfortable, yet they don't want him sedated and don't want him to die. They want him alive for the reasons we all want our parents alive, but they rarely have the time to visit him because of their own busy lives and because of the traveling distance involved.

Recently Fred developed pneumonia. Since the patient's wishes were unclear (even though he had stated many times that he wished he could "just die and get it over with"), since the family was having trouble dealing with the concept of letting him die, and since his wishes were not in writing, I had no choice but to treat the pneumonia.

Pneumonia has long been called "The Old Man's Friend." Pneumonia is no longer the old man's friend in most cases. Extremely high-potency antibiotics cure most pneumonia even in the most debilitated, terminal patients, even many of those with immune deficiency diseases. I treated Fred's pneumonia, and it cleared. I kept Fred alive so that he could return to the nursing home to lie in his feces, urine and drool and suffer 24-hour pain. He is no longer coherent or competent but is awake enough to feel his pain. I had done my job as a "good" doctor. I no longer feel that I did my job as a "complete" doctor.

● ● ●

Beth is Fred's wife. She is 84 and was placed in the nursing home because of rapidly worsening memory problems. One year prior to admission to the nursing home she had been a vibrant, sparkling, intelligent great-grandmother who had become a staring, confused individual who was never sure of what was going on around her. She had had a severe myocardial infarction (heart attack), with major damage to the heart. We had pulled her through the initial episode. Following that, her heart was markedly weakened due to the dead muscle tissue that was left behind from the clogging of her coronary arteries. Her legs began to swell, and her lungs continuously filled with fluid. Her heart could no longer pump enough blood to her brain to maintain circulation, nourishment and oxygen supply; brain function went rapidly downhill. With today's cardiac medications we can relatively easily—and on a daily basis—treat congestive heart failure, keeping the patients from drowning in their own fluid. However, we cannot reverse the damage that has been done nor can we improve beyond a certain point the pumping action of the heart. Beth, therefore, continued to deteriorate.

At first, she simply forgot recent things. Within a year she was forgetting things that had been ingrained in her brain all of her life. She forgot her home, her grandchildren, her children, and then probably her husband. Eventually she forgot everything. Not too long ago she could look at you and smile. Now she doesn't even look at you. With her head propped on a pillow, she lies in bed on continuous oxygen supplementation and has to be fed her meals. The food drools out of her mouth, down her chin and neck and onto her chest. She has a catheter to collect her urine so that it does not break down the skin of the perineum and buttocks. She has to be cleaned up several times a day because of incontinent stooling activity. She cannot lift a finger to help herself, nor can she lift a finger to defend herself. She is trying to die, but we keep attacking her with the marvels of modern-day medicine.

If we would only leave her alone and in peace, her lungs would fill with fluid within a few days, and her heart would overload and stop. But we cannot do that! It would be called neglect. Some might call it malpractice. A hot-shot prosecutor might call it murder. So we continually come to her bedside and proclaim, "I sentence you to life!"

This poor lady has been trying to die for two years. There is absolutely no hope that she can recover. There is absolutely no hope that she will even improve enough to recognize her husband, let alone enjoy a simple conversation with him or even sit and hold his hand in solitude. And yet because her wishes were never made known, because she never had a Living Will or Durable Power of Attorney for Healthcare, her family does not know what decision to make. When faced with this set of circumstances we are obliged to treat—to err on the side of conservatism—so we continue to make her live despite everything her body and nature are trying to tell us. She cannot live with dignity, and we won't let her die with dignity.

• • •

Barbara is a 78-year-old lady who was placed in the nursing home because of severe memory loss. About three and a half years ago, she came into my office with a sack full of $5, $10, $20 and $50 dollar bills and wanted me to take them because she was under the assumption that she had caused me some legal problems and wanted to make sure she paid for them. She wanted to give me all of the money in the bag, which I roughly estimated at around $800.00. I called her son, and the money was put in safekeeping. I also called her banker and informed him of the problem, to make sure that no further money was released without the family's approval—lest someone without scruples should try to get her money. At that point, Power of Attorney was signed over to her son, who had always looked out for her and her recently deceased husband.

Before she came to the nursing home, she had been doing other things, such as leaving food on the stove and boiling pans dry. Her memory since then has gone downhill quite severely. In conversation with her today, I reconfirmed that she does not know her son's name, she thinks her husband is still working on the farm, and she really has no clue as to what is going on around her. When I asked her what her birthdate was, she remembered that it was in January. When I asked her what day in January, she did what she very often does—she started to talk about one thing and simply flowed into a totally unrelated thought. She said the following: "January. Well, it is a funny name, the gal just walked in and knocked off the things she needed and put them out there and then lined them up." Even though Barbara can carry on a conversation, that conversation has no relevance to what is going on. She spends a large part of her day simply walking up and down the hallway, pacing back and forth, four or five miles a day. She is a very energetic person and is always on the move. She has gotten more and more agitated recently and has required tranquilizers to calm her down. We tried several different medications, and Mellaril® seems to work the best for her. It keeps her very calm and happy and keeps her from wandering into other residents' rooms, irritating or even hurting them when she gets angry.

On her left wrist is a "Wander-Guard™" bracelet. This is a radio-signal bracelet that sets off an alarm if she exits the nursing home. This is necessary because she wanders all day long and even at night, and she would certainly leave the building if allowed to do so. There is obviously no way she could find her way back here.

Barbara had a breast mass diagnosed in 1988, and a very loud heart murmur has evolved over the past few years. She has a severely compromised heart valve, but I believe that with her severe dementia she is not a candidate for surgery on either of these problems. Her son agrees and wishes that we institute comfort measures only. However, when she developed pneumonia last year, the family and staff wanted it treated, and we followed their wishes. At least at that time she still remembered her son's name. Now, if she develops another infection, I am not sure what the best and proper course of action will be, although if it is a simple, treatable, infectious process I suspect that the family will ask us to treat it. Soon Barbara will walk less and less, talk less and less, and shortly after that she will no longer be able to feed herself. If she develops a severe infection following that, will we again treat her? Should we again treat her?

● ● ●

Faith is an 81-year-old woman who came to the nursing home after a stroke left her with a right-sided, partial paralysis. This largely resolved only to have another major stroke leave her with total paralysis of the left side in 1988. This was permanent and associated with deteriorating mental function immediately after the stroke. She had a history of grand mal seizures and heart disease, diabetes, recurrent pneumonias and multiple other problems, including kidney failure. Faith used to be such a gregarious person. Even after her first stroke she would do knitting or needlepoint, sew articles to sell, and engage in other such activities. After her second stroke she was no longer able to do these things. Even if she might have learned to do them one-handed, she no longer has the desire to do anything. I doubt that she even has the memory to remember the stitches. She simply lies in bed or in her orthobiotic chair day in and day out, trying to catch her breath.

The staff gets her and many of the other residents up at 5:00 a.m. because there are so many people that must be gotten up before breakfast. The residents, by and large, hate this schedule. They are dragged out of bed at a time in their lives when they should be able to sleep in if they please. This is one of the necessities of an institutional schedule. They have been gotten up, cleaned and dressed and then often laid back on their bed to fall back to sleep before breakfast hour arrives. Those who can, often complain and resist, but they lose the battle every time.

Since Faith cannot move around at all, she needs to be moved by the staff. Her position is changed every two hours or she gets decubitus ulcers, commonly known as bed sores. These occur when the circulation to the skin is compressed for hours on end over a bony prominence, and the skin dies for lack of blood flow to that area. These can get so bad in some patients that the bone actually protrudes through the wound. Luckily, we have a very attentive staff at this nursing home, and we see these ulcers only rarely, although in other places I have been, the problem was severe.

As I said, Faith used to be a very gregarious person. She always used to have a joke to tell. She told me her favorite joke at least thirty times.

One day I thought she was nearly asleep, when suddenly she opened her eyes, looked at me and said, "What is the strongest part of a woman's body?" I told her that I didn't know. She said, "The chest, because it can hold two milk factories and a playground." For many months that was the only joke she could remember. Now, she doesn't tell any jokes at all.

Faith tries to feed herself, but the incoordination and weakness from the strokes cause her to drop one-third to one-half of the food onto her chest and into the towels that the staff spreads around her to catch the food. Granted, it might seem kinder to simply feed her, but if she were not forced to use her right hand, it, too, would become useless in a short period of time. She now requires three and sometimes four types of laxatives and suppository combinations to combat her severe constipation. I would not term Faith totally demented, because she can remember some things, such as the names of her sisters, one who recently died and another who is still living. She knows what year it is, but she is off by ten years as to her own age. When reminded of her age, she remarks that that is impossible. She sits and looks at the television, although I am never sure if she is really watching it, her blank stare being misleading at best. I would not term her totally unsalvageable, but she has essentially negligible rehabilitation potential. Her heart and lungs are very weak. She can barely catch her breath when attempting to speak. She is incontinent, so her stool has to be cleaned off her periodically, and she requires a catheter to drain her bladder.

We now have a glimpse of what Faith's life is like. I am not saying that it is hopeless, but I cannot say that it is hopeful. I am not saying that she has zero quality of life, but what little quality there is, most people want no part of for themselves.

• • •

Lydia is a 92-year-old lady who has suffered from schizophrenia for many years. She has been treated by various doctors over three decades for schizophrenia and has been on multiple major tranquilizers and psychotropic agents. When her husband died of lung cancer, it was impossible to even consider leaving her at home alone. He had been her caregiver, and there was no way that she could care for herself. There were times during her schizophrenic episodes that she could not carry on a reliable conversation, but as her memory has deteriorated over the last six years she can no longer carry on any conversation at all. She no longer talks, and what attempts she does make at talking are unintelligible. She is unable to feed herself and must be spoon-fed. More disconcerting than that, however, is that over the decades of ingesting medications for schizophrenia, she has developed a severe case of tardive dyskinesia. This is an involuntary muscle movement disorder that is a known side effect from chronic psychotropic drug use. It has a deleterious effect on one of the areas of the brain that is in charge of motor control and coordination. This control is lost in these patients. She is, therefore, almost paralyzed while moving at the same time. She sits slumped over in a chair, wasted away to 84 pounds. Her head always sits on her right hand—almost at a 90° angle to her waistline. This is such a chronic condition that, even though her position is changed every two hours by the staff, she immediately reverts back to "her" position so often that her right ear sticks straight out from her head because of the way she cups it in her hand. At rest she is fairly calm except for her shoulders, head and tongue, but whenever she is awakened or stimulated, her tongue begins moving continuously, usually lolling out of her mouth one to two inches in a continuous, writhing, snake-like fashion. Her jaws begin moving, her head begins swaying in uncontrollable circles and her shoulders, arms and even legs begin moving. She appears totally unaware of her surroundings and unable to interact with those surroundings or the people in her life. She does not appear to comprehend anything on television or the spoken word. She cannot feed herself and needs to be spoon-fed, but it is very difficult to feed her because of her tongue movements. She pushes out most everything that the nurses push in. They are constantly trying to time their thrusts to go along with when her tongue is fully extended. If they can hit the back of her tongue, she may swallow part of that food.

In addition, she suffers from absolutely severe constipation and requires constant laxatives, suppositories and flushing enemas. The most apt quote that I have heard came from a nurse's aid, who one day glumly summed it up: "You poke it in, then you dig it out." You see, most of these patients have very poor intake of both food and water. The stool becomes so hard and dry that it becomes impacted in balls in the rectum, and the doctors or nurses have to put on rubber gloves and dig out the hard balls of stool that are lodged in the rectal vault and cannot get through the sphincter.

This, then, is Lydia's life—paralyzed, yet constantly moving, unable to do anything for herself, unable to comprehend the world around her and unable to interact with that world.

● ● ●

Meet Charles, an 88-year-old man whose memory has been failing for approximately six to eight years. He was placed here five years ago when his weakness and memory loss made it too difficult for his wife to care for him at home any longer. At first his activities were watching television and doing a few exercises with the therapist. Very shortly, that minimal exertion declined to simply lying in bed or sitting up in the chair. He, too, is frozen into position. He cannot do anything for himself. He cannot say any words that are intelligible. He cannot even say his own name. He is totally incontinent of urine, stool and saliva and needs to be cleaned up several times a day to effect good hygiene. He was a large, strapping farmer with huge hands and powerful arms and legs. He still weighs 160 pounds, but that is only two-thirds of his prior body mass, which is going down steadily. He is now so weak and frozen into position that he has to be spoon-fed, totally unable to grasp or lift a spoon—or find his mouth if he could. Indeed, I am sure that he cannot comprehend what a spoon is any longer, nor understand what it is for. So he, too, like Lydia, has to have it "poked in and dug out."

Some of the terminal patients are at least pleasant to look at, but not Charles. He is locked in a grimace. He looks as though he has been permanently frightened. His eyes are wide and staring, and his mouth is always agape, with his teeth bared as if he is in the middle of a continuous, silent scream of terror. There is absolutely nothing we can do for him except feed him and keep him clean.

Unfortunately he gets repeated urinary tract infections whenever we have a catheter in, and this requires repeated doses of antibiotics. When he does not have a catheter in, he requires almost constant anti-yeast cream to his groin and buttock area because of the constant wetness which causes unremitting yeast growth on the skin.

Charles' weight has been dropping slowly but steadily for several years. The dietary department is, therefore, giving him high-calorie food supplements to keep his body as healthy as possible. This is a good example of what has been going on in dietary departments for the last few years. The dietitians see a series of weights, notice that the weight is going down and set out to correct "the problem." So now instead of simply forcing food down him, it is recommended that we force a protein and carbohydrate supplement down him as well, "to maintain his nutritional status." I am having more and more difficulty with that, because for individuals whose quality of life is totally unsalvageable, I am not convinced that maintaining their weight is in any way therapeutic or even desirable.

But we must continue our walk before I delve into that.

• • •

Paul is a 90-year-old man who reminds me a lot of Charles. In fact, they are so much alike in size, age and appearance that they could pass for brothers. I often have to stop and think about which one I am dealing with. Paul has suffered from Parkinson's Disease for many years. In his last years at home, he would get so confused in the middle of the night that he would be up roaming about the house, often in a violent state. He would begin tearing things up and throwing things around. Since he was a very large and strong farmer, it was very difficult for his tiny wife or even his daughter and son-in-law to control him. They began taking turns baby-sitting him at night so that he didn't tear the house apart. After one to two years of this and his worsening mental status, his wife finally had had enough. We had tried several different sedatives; the problem was that when he was not agitated he would be over-sedated, and when he was riled up there was not much that would control him. By the time the medication went to work, the agitation may have been resolved and he would sleep for twenty hours from the sedative. Eventually the family felt as though they were chasing their tails, and so they placed him in the nursing home. Since arriving here, he has continued to deteriorate in spite of optimal diet and vitamins and medication reductions. He will try to talk at times, but the words are not intelligible. He may start a word and then say part of that word ten or twenty times in a row and then cease. His arms are rigid from his Parkinson's Disease, and he cannot hold a spoon, let alone feed himself. He sits with a blank, glassy-eyed stare the few hours of the day he is awake. He is incontinent of urine and stool and always has mucous caught in his mouth and throat. He is totally unable to care for himself. He often lies in bed and groans or hollers out, requiring sedation at times so that he does not wake up other people in the wing. This has been necessary less often lately because he is in a more vegetative, nearly comatose state most of the time now.

I wish I had known Paul before he began having these problems. Before that, he was healthy and never required medical care to speak of. I also wish that I had been more aggressive years before, getting people like Paul to make their decisions about terminal care known and put down in writing. I have a great fear that I will be kept alive for years like Paul by well-intentioned people like myself.

● ● ●

Tom is a 94-year-old man who has had some memory loss for several years. About five years ago he was found to have a tumor in his large intestine, and the surgical consultant took him immediately to the operating room and removed the tumor. But you see, Tom never really woke up from the surgery. Given his condition at the time, his already demonstrable memory loss, and the fact that the tumor was very likely a slow-growing one and very possibly benign, I favored letting him live out his few remaining years in comfort, forgoing surgery and its attendant risks.

But that was not to be, and Tom was never the same after surgery. He began becoming aggressive with the nurses, at first pinching their nipples or caressing their behinds whenever he got the chance. Then, as time went on, he became downright belligerent, at first swearing at them, then later hitting the staff when they tried to work with him. This has gotten to the point that the staff either wants him sedated or they refuse to work with him, a condition which is at odds with his wife's wish that he not be sedated.

Ten years ago Tom would never have thought of abusing a nurse, but a few months ago he scored a near knock-out with a solid blow to the jaw of a nurse when she was giving him a bath. He would have been embarrassed at best—more likely, ashamed—if he had known he was pinching at breasts and buttocks, making lewd comments along the way. But now he no longer does this, not because he has improved, but because he can barely talk at all anymore. He can still hit and holler, though, and continues to do so in his pain every time he is moved.

He is in pain every day now, his rectum aflame with bleeding hemorrhoids from his constant and severe constipation, his joints frozen from inactivity and arthritis, his hips and ankles now oozing from paper-thin skin breaking open over the bony prominences of the femur and fibula. But he is alive! We have succeeded!

Five years ago he asked that we let him die. "Leave me ALONE" he would holler, so loud you could hear him around the corner, down the hallway and into the cafeteria. But we couldn't leave him alone. He was demented and raving. He had to be. No one in his right mind would want to die. Since what we do for people is the "right" thing, it only follows that anyone refusing our help is sick and unable to make the "right" choice. So we ignored Tom's wishes to be left alone to die, just as we ignore hundreds and thousands of people's wishes each year. Since it is "normal" to choose life over death, since that is a built-in survival instinct, it is assumed naturally, as a matter of course, that those doing otherwise must be out of their senses. So we declare them incompetent and force our care upon them. The only problem is that there are no 95-year-olds making these administrative decisions. Their outlook at the end of life, their instinct for survival at that age, their views, wishes, and rights aren't even considered. Who is talking to them? Who is talking for them?

● ● ●

Martha is an 83-year-old lady who just a few years ago was a very intelligent, self-educated person. She would read and travel. Remembering my very first encounter with her some ten years ago, I recall how well-read she was about her medical problems. However, over the past few years her memory became so poor that her husband could not leave her at home; and since he continued to operate his own business, he could not stay with her. He would come home to find things burning on the stove. Toward the end of her home care she would wander and become lost. Finally, one day she fell in her kitchen and sustained a pelvic fracture and a hip dislocation, and her husband simply could not take care of her any longer. In fact, the children were more worried about him at that stage, because he was wearing himself out caring for her.

Martha has also had heart problems and severe arthritis and has had gastrointestinal bleeding from the ingestion of so much arthritis medication. Her main problem, however, is her severe degenerative cerebral function. She now only lies in bed or sits in her chair. When asked today whether she has any problems with memory, she stated that she used to have such problems, but that was when she was younger. As she tried to explain it, she went into detail about how her dress was not fitting right even though she had just fixed it. She floats from subject to subject without knowing she is doing so and without its bothering her in the least. She is still able to feed herself, although it is a very, very slow process and worsening. She no longer walks and is now constantly battling decubitus ulcers over the coccyx (tailbone) area.

The most disconcerting thing about Martha is that she is constantly hollering. She is at the far end of the south wing where she will bother the fewest people, yet you can often hear her in the north wing hollering, "Nurse, Nurse, Nurse!

Won't somebody help me?" If you ask her what she needs, she cannot remember. Most often she will say that she has to go to the bathroom even though she may have just returned from there five minutes ago. Recently we put a catheter in her bladder, but she cannot remember that she has a catheter, so she continues to holler for the nurse to take her to the bathroom. A few weeks ago when I spoke with her she could not remember her son's name, and as I visited with her today in preparing these notes, she could no longer remember her husband's name, either. She no longer walks, and soon she will not be able to feed herself. Shortly after that she will quit talking and then will lie in bed or in her orthobiotic chair, and the staff will "poke it in and dig it out." If she is lucky, her heart will stop quietly in the middle of the night and she will be spared any more degradation.

● ● ●

Jessica is a 90-year-old lady whom I never met before her stroke. She had lived in our community in years past and was moved back here to our nursing home following her most recent stroke. She has been absolutely devastated by a series of strokes, with a resultant paralysis of all four extremities and the most severe contractures I have seen. Her hips curl up and her legs curl back so that her knees are always up in the air. Her elbows are contractured up toward her chest and her hands are so contractured that they gouge her palms. If her fingernails are not cut, they dig into her flesh. Her face is in a constant grimace, and she seems to be in continuous pain from being locked in this horrendous position. She will often look at you if you speak to her, but it is a look of fear. As she looks at you, she tries to move her head away, as if she is going to be struck. If you move her, she screams. Her screaming makes Martha's hollering for help seem quiet. These are blood-curdling screams that make people in the hallway think someone is torturing her. They are so loud that she has been moved to the far end room and so loud that if I dictate in the hallway from fifty feet away, my typist will be able to hear the screams coming over the tiny dictaphone's speaker. Jessica does not know she is hollering, of course. She cannot help it. She does not understand that she keeps people awake at night and, therefore, needs to be sedated periodically. Sedation is necessary, not just because other residents need to sleep, but also because Jessica needs pain relief.

She, like most of the others, is difficult to feed, but the staff gets the job done right. It is one thing to do a job right. It is entirely another question to know if you are doing the right job.

● ● ●

Mabel, an 82-year-old woman, has had a much more rapid decline than most of the patients we normally see with senile dementia of the Alzheimer's type. She had been very robust and energetic up until a year ago, when her daughter noticed that she was starting to forget things. Within just a few weeks she was no longer able to fix meals or clean her house and required the County Health Nurse and Homemaker Aide services in her home. Within just a few months she was to the point at which they did not trust leaving her at home. Her memory loss has been dramatic and severe, both in amount and speed of onset. Now when we talk, she looks at us with a profoundly confused look on her face, and her gait is becoming shuffling in a Parkinsonian fashion. She already requires help walking.

Mabel had a huge family and has multiple scrapbooks with family pictures in them. She used to sit and look at these scrapbooks for hours, but now no longer can identify family members in pictures and cannot remember the names of her own children. There has been barely a year since this onset, and I doubt that in six months she will be able to do anything for herself. Her current life has little, if anything, to offer and her former life simply does not exist anymore—not even in her memories.

● ● ●

Myrtle's case is similar to Mabel's. Myrtle now lives like Mabel will undoubtedly be living within the year. She has been unable to remember her children's names for four to five years and she no longer interacts with her surroundings. She simply holds onto her pink teddy bear and smiles off into space. Until about a year ago she at least tried to carry on a conversation, faking it as she went along because she could not remember facts to put into the conversation. All she now seems able to remember is her own name and her pink teddy bear. Myrtle's condition is typical of the end stages of existence of most of these patients, right down to the fact that she made no provisions for her terminal care and has no Living Will or Durable Power of Attorney for Healthcare. If she develops a "treatable" illness, then the pressure will be on the family to make a decision—something families are not often well prepared to do because of lack of exposure and experience. So if they are like most families, they will elect to treat, to try to "take care" of Myrtle as long as they can. You see, it is standard and customary in this country to treat while we can treat. We simply don't ask the question, will it improve their quality of life or simply prolong it? Will it prolong their living or prolong their dying?

● ● ●

Hilda is a 102-year-old, superb lady who, up until three years ago, was in the nursing home simply because of weakness and blindness. She was the one person I consistently looked forward to seeing on rounds because, even though she could not see me, she could recognize my voice from the doorway and sit and talk about the old days. She would always say that she was so grateful that she had her wits about her. Every single time we talked she would philosophize on how we had to be patient with the residents who would wander into her room and get into her things because, "They don't know what they're doing." She would go on to say how she was so grateful that God had left her with her mind, even though He had taken her strength and vision.

Just before her 100th birthday, Hilda started going downhill fairly rapidly in terms of memory loss and then began having grand mal seizures.

As time went on, she began forgetting almost everything and eventually quit talking. She now no longer converses but lies in bed saying, "Goodness me," and asking for "Mommy" and "Daddy." She is totally unable to eat on her own. She is, therefore, spoon-fed what she can swallow. Although a small person to begin with, she is now wasted to a total of 63 pounds. She has not walked in three years and is also now suffering from the ravages of skin cancers that are eating away at the side of her cheek and nose. We have arrested those with electrocautery surgery so that they are no longer continuously draining and bleeding, but it is only a matter of time before they do so again. Hilda also suffers from congestive heart failure and requires heart medications daily, without which she would undoubtedly die. More recently she has become more and more confused and agitated. She has been requiring Thorazine® in children's dosages to keep her from awakening her roommate and other people in her hallway. She requires periodic catheterization of the bladder to keep the urine off of her skin, but if the catheter is left in too long, she gets infections.

The sum total of her day now amounts to lying in bed sleeping about twenty-three hours a day and getting up into a chair and sleeping in the chair for an hour. What she does eat is spoon-fed to her, half of it running down her chin. The other half turns into constipated stool, requiring laxatives to keep her bowels emptying regularly. She has no interaction that could be considered intelligible by or with anyone. What interaction she tries to have at this point in time is based on her childhood experiences, because she simply calls out for her parents. She recognizes no one and rarely has visitors. She is essentially in a state of semi-comatose existence. She told me so many times over the years that she was ready to die, that she had lived a long life and a good life and she just wished that she could die before she lost her mind. Now, even that has been denied her. Like Beth, she cannot live with dignity, and the question I have to ask myself is, "Can I let her die with dignity?" Since she gave no advance directives, we can only rely on the family. The question now is what to do if she gets a treatable illness such as an infection. Is it good medicine to treat the infection, or is it better medicine to ignore the infection, given this set of circumstances?

Last year Hilda was brought to our hospital because of a severe urinary tract infection—one that easily could have taken her life. The family would not make a decision to not treat. They felt as though they should do something. Having no Living Will or Durable Power of Attorney, we were forced to admit her, cure her, and in the words of one of my nurses, "Send her back to the home to die some more!" I know in my heart what Hilda would have wanted. Our conversations over the last thirteen years convinced me completely that she dreaded this demise worse than death. She said time and again that she was ready to die. She had lived a long and happy life, and there was nothing left to do. The only thing she looked forward to anymore was seeing God. Yet, without written directions, I could be sued for malpractice, manslaughter or murder if I treated her only with comfort measures in the face of a life-threatening infection. I cannot and will not jeopardize my future and my family's future to let a Hilda die without written authorization—not with the sad state of affairs that our legal system is in today. No, I will take care of the Hildas. I will keep them alive when they deserve to die quickly and with dignity, and I will get paid well for it, but I won't feel particularly good about it.

Hilda was such a proud and graceful lady and dreaded this day for years. Now if she knew she was on welfare and was what she thought of as a burden on the taxpayers, she would feel even worse. I know what she wanted and I know what I would want if I were Hilda. The question is, "What can I do?"

● ● ●

Dora is an 89-year-old woman who, a few years ago, was the epitome of grace, elegance and class. She was involved in politics well into her eighties, extremely knowledgeable, well-read, and active. Never did I hear a harsh word cross her lips nor an unkind thought expressed publicly or privately. Two years ago she began having slight lapses of memory and started becoming more and more confused. She wasn't able to complete sentences or carry on a decent conversation. The night she was admitted to the nursing home she was even unable to eat. Her condition had worsened rapidly that evening. It appeared that she had had an acute stroke, which caused sudden worsening of her recent memory loss and confusion. She also suffers from congestive heart failure, which followed a heart attack in 1988, as well as several other problems.

In contrast to the 86-year-old, elegant lady I so recently knew, I am now looking at an 89-year-old lady with a confused look on her face who cannot find her own room. She packs her clothes several times a day because she is going home. Right after the staff puts her things away, she starts folding and packing them again. When she is told that she must stay here, she gets very sad. When she asks for her car keys, she is told that her car is at the shop, and she says that she will stay here a few days until it is fixed.

She always dresses neatly. She has always had great pride in her appearance. Although she knew me well for many years as I cared for her dying sister, she no longer recognizes me nor knows my name. She seems to recognize her family, but when asked to come up with their names on her own, she cannot do so. She does vaguely remember her home and cries when told she can no longer return there.

While not actually terminal in the usual sense of the word, this lady's mental status is poor and irreversible. She, however, signed a Durable Power of Attorney document that allows her nephew to make decisions for her medical care when she is unable to do so. She specifically has requested in her Durable Power of Attorney that no life sustaining or prolonging treatments be used if she is in a coma or has an incurable or terminal condition. That was the way Dora was—always organized, always on top of things. Now she has set the stage for her terminal care, taking the burden off the family and making her wishes perfectly clear. When she worsens, she will not be "saved" from a condition that can take her life, only to suffer the slow demise experienced by the others you have met here today.

2

PATIENTS' WISHES
AND PATIENTS' RIGHTS

THE PATIENTS YOU HAVE JUST MET are real. I have not exaggerated or embellished any of this. Indeed, I had planned to be much more graphic, to include more of the sights and sounds and smells of this hallway, but good taste and sensitivity for their families prompted me to tone down the descriptors somewhat. Nonetheless, the state of helplessness and hopelessness of these elderly people is graphic to those of us who must care for them daily.

I use the words helplessness and hopelessness very purposefully. The patients feel the helplessness. They hate it when it first starts. They do not go into nursing homes readily. Contrary to what many younger people seem to think, the desire for independence does not vanish with age. Many—by far, most—families try to take over their elders' care as if older people cannot express an opinion or be a critical part of their own plans. The family sees some failure at self care and moves in, usually with the best intentions, and tries to force the loved one into a nursing home. I have rarely seen even a hint of families, in the Midwest at least, trying to misappropriate their parents' funds. It is simply that they wish them to be clean and safe and well cared for.

We hear more and more about cases where the courts have intervened in a patient's wish to refuse care and die quickly. It is my premise that the courts are as misguided by "good intentions" as the families themselves. The overriding factor in many court decisions has been to err on the conservative side—to choose life over death.

But what about the patients themselves? What about their wishes? What about their rights?

We must now ask the question, "Are we really prolonging life, or are we prolonging death?" And ultimately, "Who really has the right to make that decision?" We are not—and I emphasize, NOT—talking about suicide or physician-assisted euthanasia. We are talking about human beings who are facing the most certain thing in life, and that is that we all shall die. These people are actually in the process of dying. They are beyond our help. Their hearts, lungs, livers and kidneys may be working, but their brains—the very essence of who they are—no longer function to any degree that we would call human. So, are they alive? Yes, technically, but what is that life? A body lying in a pool of urine and feces, unable to even comprehend their incontinence, let alone enjoy a conversation. Many cannot even pick up a spoon to feed themselves. Once they have reached this stage they obviously cannot make their own end-of-life decisions. So it is left to families, doctors, nurses and court-appointed patient representatives with Powers of Attorney to decide. It is this very step where the principle problem lies. It is the process of placing the decision-making power in the hands of third person committees that makes it nearly impossible to do what I now believe is the right thing. Once a disinterested third party is involved, they find it nearly impossible to withhold treatment. They will, almost without question, do what the doctors recommend, and doctors are trained to treat illness! Indeed, it is because of the successes of modern medicine that we have so many elderly in nursing homes today—some 1.4 million, with somewhere between 600,000 and one million partially or totally demented.

Doctors are now finding it easier to withhold major surgery, respirators and the like, but most seem unwilling to withhold simpler, more conventional treatments. A national survey of doctors published in the summer of 1991 showed that the younger doctors were more likely to allow the patient to decide, but the numbers were just over 60% for certain things. Isn't it time we asked, "What does the patient want?"

By 1985, I was asking myself that question over and over. I was seeing a consistent—shall I say "overwhelming"—pattern to my practice. When I had to rely on families or patient representatives for direction, the answer usually was not forthcoming, or the answer was to go ahead and treat because of their uncertainty. But every individual patient I talked to—every patient of mine—said that they hoped that I or someone would let them die if they were in a persistent mental condition that precluded any reasonable quality of life and had no reasonable hope of recovery. **This was 100% in my practice.** I knew what I wanted. I knew what all of my family wanted. I knew what every one of my patients with whom I had talked about this subject wanted. Yet courts and court-appointed representatives could not make these decisions. I came to believe that the reason they could not make these decisions was because, too often, they were non-medical people who lacked the training and background to be placed in the position they were in. They had often been appointed to watch over financial matters and were now asked to make medical-ethics decisions which they were not trained or experienced to make. So it was in 1985 that I started my own poll to see what the people really wanted. I purposely did not use my own patients for this portion of the study. I felt that my close relationship would taint the validity of the poll. Critics could say that I held too much sway over their decision making. Therefore, when I went to Minneapolis, Minnesota, for a week of cardiology updating, I went to two different shopping malls in my off hours and polled people at random. I polled young and old, black and white, male and female.

I wish that I could say that the poll matched with 100% concordance the results of my local patient population, but two answers out of three hundred and fifty left me short of that 100% concordance, by 0.57%. This confirmed what I knew from my practice. When given the choice, virtually no one wants to be kept alive when they are beyond hope. The questionnaire had six questions which read as follows:

1. If you were severely brain damaged for a prolonged period of time and there was no reasonable hope for recovery, would you want your family to keep you alive with artificial devices? No___ Yes___

2. If you were severely brain damaged for a prolonged period of time and there was no reasonable hope of recovery, would you want your family to place a plastic tube down your nose or through your stomach and have feedings given indefinitely through the tube? No___ Yes___

3. Under these circumstances would you ask your family to let you die by withholding feedings and water if it was quite certain that you would not feel anything? No___ Yes___

4. Do you believe that people should have the right to refuse these types of life sustaining measures and devices in advance? No___ Yes___

5. Do you consider feeding by a plastic tube to be a "natural" (as opposed to "artificial") means of feeding? No___ Yes___

6. Do you believe the government should have the power to force families to keep brain damaged people alive by tube feedings? No____ Yes____

The answers were nearly 100% in favor of self determination and the right to die. One lady pondered the question on tube feedings and said, "I don't think anyone should starve to death, so I think I would have to say 'Yes' to feedings." However, she had answered that she did not want to be kept alive by artificial devices. She would not want a tube placed down her nose or through her stomach. Hers was the only one that was confusing to figure out because she felt that people should have the right to choose, free of government intervention, and she, herself, didn't want to be kept alive; yet she was unsure about feedings and water. I will speak more to that in the next few pages. The second person stated that she would ask her family to withhold feedings but not water. In both of these cases there was the desire for a quick and dignified death, yet there was confusion over what could or should be done. I wonder, since they answered five of six questions in favor of a dignified death, what their answers would have been if they had watched several dozen people die a slow and probably painful death because they were kept "alive" by artificial feedings? What would they have said if they had watched loved ones shrivel away to nothing by the slow starvation of inadequate feedings compounded by their body's inability to digest and utilize what was being fed them? I know what all of my medical staff want after taking care of Hildas and Lydias and Marthas.

I did this survey myself. I felt it important that I ask all the questions personally, so that I could be confident that each respondent understood the questions. Just as in my own general practice of more than four thousand patients, none of the shopping mall respondents even hesitated in answering the other questions. After conducting that survey, I have begun to encourage more and more people to make their wishes known in advance. Too often they feel uncomfortable in bringing up the subject, and most doctors are, likewise, uncomfortable in approaching the patient about the subject. As I have been more active in this arena, I have become more convinced that the feeling expressed by those I've questioned is a universal desire. I have never met anyone who wants to be kept alive artificially beyond their productive, brain-healthy years. In fact, it goes well beyond that. Everyone *wishes* for a quick, clean death.

Another common misconception is found in the presumption that the very elderly fear death. I know from personal experience that this is usually not the case. Most very elderly have come to grips with the inevitability of their death and have come to accept it. Because of their age, they know it is imminent. In fact, many (those who are not healthy or are in a lot of pain) wish for it. It is more common than not to hear comments such as, "Just let me die," or, "Can't you just give me a shot so I can go to sleep and not wake up?" These people readily sign statements that state their final wishes for "comfort and pain measures only," "no CPR" and "no artificial life support, including feedings." They sit in the nursing home, seeing Freds, Beths and Lydias on a daily basis, and hope—and yes, even pray—that they will die quickly, in order to avoid that worst of afflictions, Living Death.

• • •

Bill is 85 years old and is suffering from kidney failure. It is currently in it's final stages, and he is certain to be dead before this book is completed. Three months ago I told him what the problem was and why he was so weak; I asked him if he wanted to consider renal dialysis.

Bill had been a railroad worker all of his life. He looked me squarely in the eye and said, "This car has traveled down a long track, and that track is coming to an end. It is time to change tracks now." Bill refused all treatment so that he could die peacefully. He wanted no part of needles and tubes and IVs and trips to the dialysis unit sixty-five miles away. He was totally competent to make that decision. I absolutely believe that he had every right to do so. No committee to decide for him. No doctors forcing or coercing him to accept treatment. No "misinformed consent" to tell him half truths so he would acquiesce to treatment. I gave him full disclosure, and he made the same decision I would have made at 85—not 25 or 45, or even 65, perhaps. But at 85, dialysis does not work well or for long. So this unique individual, with his unique set of circumstances, took the information and acted upon it. Who dares to say he was wrong to accept his fate? Who dares to say it would be better to try for a few more months of potentially painful, miserable weakness and of feeling sickly most of the time? Who could possibly be in a better position than he to make that decision? He is now so weak he can barely get out of bed. His brain function is not what it was even three weeks ago. I am not sure that he could be considered mentally competent at this writing. What if I had withheld his right to make his own decision while he was still competent to do so? Could I have been sure that I knew what was best or right for him? And if a court had appointed a guardian, how would that person have known any better than I?

Yes, Bill is dying, but he is satisfied that it is coming quickly.

If all of us are like Bill—and I feel that we are—and if all of us want a peaceful death with some semblance of dignity, why is it that as a society we have such trouble making the transition when a third party is the one who is dying? I believe in my heart that it is because the wrong people are now in charge of making those decisions. Well-intentioned though they may be, the courts have neither the medical training nor the firsthand experience necessary to do so. It is up to you to make sure your own wishes are fulfilled.

Could anyone say that Bill did not have the right to make his own decisions? Yes, there are those people out there who feel that they have God's blessing in telling others what is right. Such people forbade Nancy Cruzan the right to refuse tube feedings and hydration. Such people forbade Karen Ann Quinlan's parents from unplugging her respirator. Such people are so certain of their knowledge of what God wants that they want to make your decisions for you! I hope that this scares you just a little bit. These are the same types of people who burned women alive because of the certainty that they were witches and tortured others to death to "save" them from their possession by the devil. Be wary of those who have all the answers and are too self-righteous in their rightness.

One of the things that has made America what it is today is our underlying belief in personal freedom. It is at the root of all the major court decisions that have shaped this country's system of jurisprudence. Of key importance in this philosophy of personal independence is the concept of self-determination. Courts have traditionally and repeatedly upheld the citizen's right to self-determination in almost all matters. I say "almost all" and not "all" because of a few cases like Nancy Cruzan's, in which lower courts have ordered the institution or continuation of feedings. The Supreme Court seems to be coming closer and closer to the determination that individuals have the ultimate right to make end-of-life decisions for themselves. Now that the **Patient Self-Determination Act of 1990** has been enacted by the Congress, a positive direction has been set by both the legislative and the judicial branches. Finally.

This is a somewhat new area, in fact, because before the technology existed to keep people alive for long periods, the question had really never come up. As members of society have become more and more sophisticated in addressing these issues—coming to demand more control over their destinies—the courts have become more prone to allow self-determination. For example, a poll completed in August of 1991 showed that, although more than 60% of respondents did not feel that abortion was right for them, more than 60% also felt that it had to be an individual, private decision and were opposed to militant anti-abortionists using physical means to close or hamper abortion clinics. The citizenry is proclaiming that people should have the right to determine how they live, given the technological advances of the day. They do not feel that it has to be right for them to be right for someone else. They are simply reaffirming the American belief in freedom of choice and self-determination.

So if, after these polls and this discussion, we now have a glimpse of what people want and we know what their rights are, where is the problem? The problem begins when people do not make their wishes known—in writing—while they are still competent! Once it is in the hands of third parties, it becomes difficult to make the jump from, "what I would want" to "what we should do for patient X." It is very hard for others to "choose death" over life for someone else. It is only when they know what that life would be like, only when they have seen hundreds of people die a slow and humiliating death, that they start to make that transition. That transition at one time was hard to make for people kept alive by respirators. When the technology was new, families—and, indeed, doctors— thought that given time on the respirator, the injuries would possibly heal, and these patients would recover. This is true for certain injuries. Hearts heal, lungs heal, livers heal because they have a simple function and can work on partial tissue. The brain has to work as a complete entity, or it does not work as it did before the injury. It is too complex an organ, and it requires too much interaction with its various parts, to simply "heal up" like a liver, spleen or lung. Therefore, when people began seeing and realizing that brain-damaged people were not going to recover, it started becoming easier for doctors and families to turn off respirators. This was not always the case, however. When the technology was new, it was difficult for people to accept this, especially the families. They saw the patient alive and breathing and warm, and they held on to hope beyond hope that their loved one would recover. It is now commonplace for families to fully understand the concept of brain death and to agree to cessation of artificial respiration once all hope is gone. But letting go of other forms of artificial life support is not only difficult, the thought is usually not even entertained.

I have watched many people die. I have watched them die quickly, and I have watched them die slowly. I have many examples of real-life patients I could show you, but the case of David portrays all of the problems of patients' wishes and, even more so, patients' rights better than any theoretical scenario I could make up.

• • •

David was a 32-year-old serviceman who was riding his motorcycle one beautiful summer day when he lost control of the bike. He sustained multiple bodily injuries, major fractures and, unfortunately, irreversible brain damage. The military hospital did all of the usual life-saving maneuvers—tracheostomy, feeding tubes, IV fluids and multiple operations to repair broken bones and sew up or remove torn organs. They then performed multiple additional operations to try to restore some semblance of human appearance to the face that had been ripped away in the accident. However, through all of this, David never regained any brain function beyond very primitive brainstem reflexes. When there were no more operations to be done, they placed a feeding tube through a hole in his abdominal wall and discharged him from the service. He was brought back to South Dakota and placed in our nursing home.

On examination, David was a twisted, wasting white male who could only grimace in apparent pain when moved. His arms and legs had multiple fractures and were twisted and contracted. They could neither flex nor extend. Stainless steel pins still protruded from one of his legs. His muscles were wasted, and what little subcutaneous fat he once might have had was gone. You could count his ribs from ten feet away. Part of his face was gone—the left eye missing, a huge piece of cheek bone and skull bone absent—leaving a horrifying depression that made most people stop and gape when they first saw him. Worst of all was the lack of brain activity as we know it. He was not "brain dead" in the true sense of the electro-encephalogram definition. His brain stem functioned enough to control his respirations and temperature. Beyond that, there was no evidence that he heard his family, saw his family or recognized them if he did. There was only the grimace of pain every time he was moved and the constant dribble of urine, feces and saliva.

And the gurgling!

His brain could not tell when his throat was full of saliva and phlegm, so he could not cough or swallow to get rid of it. He gurgled and choked almost hourly on his own secretions, requiring constant suctioning by the nursing staff.

And last there was the feeding tube protruding from a small hole in the upper abdominal wall—man's gift of life to this poor soul whom the gods had long ago forsaken.

David was not trying to live; he was trying to die. And except for the advances of modern medicine, he would have died months earlier.

I am not in any slightest fashion implying that life-saving technologies should not have been used on David. Many people who would have died thirty years ago are alive and living happy, productive lives today because of the advances in medicine. We never know the extent of brain damage initially; therefore, we go all out in the emergency setting. What we don't do well is decide when to quit. That is exactly what happened with David. If anyone was trying to die, it was surely he.

Within a few months of arrival at our facility, he was more wasted, more contracted and in more evident pain than before. I had been wrestling with the dilemma to do what a "good" doctor would do and what a "complete" doctor should do when Mother Nature handed me the opening. With all wounds, the body's natural healing and defense mechanisms continually work to seal them shut. So it was with David's feeding jejunostomy. At first it was a little difficult to replace the tube when it got a month old and began caking and plugging. Then it got very difficult. Then the opening got so small that I had to insert spreading forceps and manually force it open. Eventually, I could no longer get a tube into the pinhole opening.

From my experience I know that most doctors would simply have scheduled an appointment in the operating room schedule and made a larger opening—going about the business of "caring" for David's life. But since I cared about David, I met with his parents, instead. It was at that point that I made the decision to break with tradition and follow my conscience. I told them what the procedure would entail (informed consent). Then I told them that it would keep David alive, perhaps, if repeated often enough, for years. Then I told them what they already knew—what his chances of recovery were two years after the accident. Then I posed the most simple, and yet in retrospect the most profound question that I could have asked. I asked them if they wanted me to operate or let nature take its course.

His parents were momentarily stunned and

speechless. They conversed between themselves and then looked at me and said, "We didn't know we had a choice!" Suddenly everything I had suspected about terminal medical care was confirmed. As we talked into the afternoon, it came to light that the family had never once been consulted. They had often not been told by the V.A. doctors what had been done even after it was done. And nowhere was there a mention of choice.

They had secretly felt that their son had been a "nonperson," a military entity, a guinea pig for V.A. surgical residents' practice, but they had no experience on which to draw, no enlightenment into the process by which to question David's care. They simply waited passively for a miracle to happen—for him to wake up. I then told them that I firmly believed that they and the other immediate family members were the only ones who could speak for David, that they were the ones who knew as well as anyone could know what David would have wanted for himself under these circumstances. And then I told them what I would want if I were the patient, or if it were my parent or brother or son. Suddenly they were in control—empowered with a new set of rules, if you will. I asked them to return home, to call together David's brothers and sisters, and to come to a consensus. I told them that I would do whatever the family directed me to do, so long as there was 100% agreement. And I required that it be put down in writing and signed by all of them.

Take a moment now and reflect. What would

you have done for your brother, your son or your father? They made the decision that I knew in my heart they would make, having watched them grieve over David for months. His older brother took the lead at our family conference.

"David was a free spirit. He would never want to be kept alive in this condition. If he couldn't be really alive, he would rather be dead."

No one disagreed. No one even hinted that there was another choice. His father gave me a handwritten letter signed by all members of the immediate family, authorizing me to withhold replacement of the feeding tube. For the first few days the nursing staff tried to give David food and water by mouth, but he could not swallow it. He continually choked on it, and finally, after about four days, the mother requested that we no longer do even that because it seemed to bother him so much, making him constantly cough and choke. David died four days later.

Ironically perhaps to some, but not to me, there was an end to the family's sorrow and suffering, just as there was an end to David's. You see, he had been dead for months, and they had already grieved enough. Now, they actually had a feeling of relief. They had helped put an end to his suffering as well. And I have never looked back. I have never felt even a moment's reluctance at what I had done. I was his doctor, in the most complete sense I can imagine. In fact, I only look back now with a fond sense of farewell, and a job well done.

In this debate you will hear that starving a person to death is inhumane, and I agree. But we did not starve David to death. No one starves to death in four days. David died of dehydration, as well as his chronic malnutrition. People will say that starving to death is slow and painful. That is probably true, but what about dehydration? This question must be addressed now, once and for all.

Sickly humans die of starvation in thirty to sixty days, of dehydration in three to six days. I have witnessed, time and again, a physician labeling someone as terminal and then placing the patient on intravenous fluids for their "comfort." Doctors do this in the mistaken thought that dying of dehydration is worse than dying of starvation. Now stop and ask yourself, would you rather die in four days or forty?— forty days or four thousand? Is there even a choice?

I personally, based on years of experience of overseeing people die from various maladies, believe that there is very little discomfort, let alone suffering, from a death due to dehydration. Again, remind yourself that we are not talking of healthy people committing suicide, but of already brain-damaged people who don't comprehend their surroundings. Certainly, the thought of a 24-year-old, healthy person dying in the desert is not pleasant, but it is my experience that brain-damaged people do not feel any difference when fluids are withheld. Their facial countenance does not change. Their reflex activity does not indicate that they are in pain. In fact, they simply slip deeper and deeper into coma—the dying person's natural escape from pain and suffering. Within a few days they are gone. This is not cruel; it is kind. This is not euthanasia; it is recognizing our limitations and acknowledging the point at which we can do no more. It is letting go—letting nature take its course. We will all die. It is my conviction that we each have the right to decide, within our power to do so, if we will die with dignity.

3

THE GLOBAL PICTURE

I AM CERTAIN TO BE CRITICIZED by some for "choosing death" instead of "choosing life." But I must repeat: this is not a book on mercy-killing, euthanasia or doctor-assisted suicide. There are no overdoses of sleeping pills here, no intravenous boluses of potassium chloride or morphine sulfate. In this play, death has already been chosen for the players as it someday will be for us. It is not only beyond anyone's power to stop the process in these people, but in fact the dying has progressed through most of the brain already, so we are not "choosing" death for them; we are simply in charge of overseeing it. I have come to believe through first-hand observations that in this area, half measures are worse than no measures. If there is nothing we can do, then we must be brave enough not to do anything.

My overriding concerns in writing about this are the patient's rights, the patient's dignity, and the patient's and family's suffering. Those alone are what really matter. There are other factors involved, to be sure. As this world gets overpopulated, which it already is, we find ourselves facing decisions that society never faced even one generation ago. When there seemed to be unlimited land and unlimited resources, prioritization did not seem necessary. Again, I repeat: the technology of the past thirty years has enabled us to keep people alive so much longer that we as a society must start asking ourselves what our priorities will be.

Americans over the age of 65 account for only approximately 11% of our population, but they take up 40% of our acute hospital bed days. This group uses up approximately 30% of our total national health budget and accounts for more than 50% of the 253 billion dollar federal and state health budget. Nursing home care alone costs approximately 75 billion dollars a year. There are currently 1,491,000 patients in nursing homes. Depending on the level of memory impairment used to define dementia in different studies, anywhere from 50 to 70% of these people suffer from dementia. It is the number one reason people are admitted to a nursing home, since they can no longer care for themselves. In addition to the drain on national resources, I have watched families financially devastated by the costs of terminal care. I have seen comfortable nest eggs eaten up on the terminal care of one spouse, only to leave the healthy one destitute and on welfare. What has that accomplished? They had to watch their spouse linger and watch their savings go up in smoke at the same time. This situation is often the cause of significant depression.

What have I to gain by promoting "benign

neglect" in these patients? I can make perfectly good money on these patients. With good documentation one can be reimbursed quite nicely for "caring" for these patients, and the risk is very low because they are expected to die anyway. Therefore if the outcome is not good, no one is disappointed; it was not anticipated that you could work miracles in the first place. If all I wanted to do was make money, I would simply continue to care for them in the absolute best fashion that modern medicine has to offer. I am finding, however, that I can no longer do that in good conscience. There are doctors and hospitals who make thousands of extra dollars on such patients, doing procedures that will make no difference in their outcome. I have even been told by experienced RNs of their firsthand experiences with doctors who, when things are slow, go and "flush" their nursing homes to fill hospital beds. I don't doubt that this happens. I know it would be so easy. It is such easy money and impossible to track. There is always the appearance of "good medicine." In fact, I have an ongoing conversation with my nursing home RNs about this subject, so that we are always on guard against unwarranted admissions. Just because you can do something doesn't mean that you should!

Where should our priorities lie when $50,000 to $250,000 can be spent in one year on a brain dead person, and a child in the ghetto cannot get three decent meals a day or an education that could keep him off the welfare rolls in 20 years?

Another bothersome statistic is that, of the $250,000,000,000 spent yearly by just the federal and state health budgets, one-third ($83,000,000,000) will be spent on individuals who will die that year. It is time to ask ourselves how many of these were terminal when they were admitted? How many of these presented no hope of salvage in the first place? How many of these people wanted to be left alone to die in peace?

There are those who will say that we would wreak havoc in the nursing home and hospital job market if we "let go." Why not shift the priority and create the same number of jobs in taking care of the healthy? Let's make a difference in the life of someone who has a life yet to live! Let's truly "choose life."

Personally, I do not want to be a beneficiary of that kind of waste of resources when there are so many inequities in the world. To waste thousands of dollars on me when it is too late, when some child could be eating and growing and learning and living life instead of dying of disease and starvation, is more than distasteful to me. It is immoral. I feel guilty when I waste a small bowl of potatoes, when people all around the world are starving. How then can I justify hundreds of thousands of dollars on my own care when my brain is not even there to appreciate it? I cannot live with it. I will not live with it. I choose to declare my right to self-determination and fulfill my final responsibility to society. I refuse to waste resources that rightfully belong to the next generation, that could be used for someone who could truly benefit from them. This is my final act of social responsibility, and if one million other people in this country alone did the same, we could help feed, clothe, and educate all of the disadvantaged children in America.

4

THE LIVING WILL AND THE DURABLE POWER OF ATTORNEY FOR HEALTHCARE

THERE IS ONLY ONE WAY you, as an individual, can hope to assure that your final wishes are carried out in this all-important matter: that is to do it now, while you are still competent, and to do it in writing. There are two vehicles by which this may be done: the **Living Will** and the **Durable Power of Attorney for Healthcare**. I advocate the use of both, so that there can be no doubt about your wishes and directives.

In 1985, shortly after David's death, I began lobbying for Living Will legislation in South Dakota. I wrote letters to all of the state representatives and senators urging that patients, families and healthcare providers alike be provided with this tool for making end-of-life decisions easier for healthcare providers and, especially, for families. Legislation was tabled year after year. No one wanted to tackle an issue that, to me, was clear-cut from the beginning. Why this reluctance? I suspect it is because the legislators, being untrained and inexperienced in these matters, were uncomfortable making these decisions for others—exactly as families and court-appointed designees are uncomfortable making them for third parties.

California was the first state to recognize by law a Living Will in 1976, the same year that the Karen Ann Quinlan case was decided in New Jersey. Currently, forty- six states and the District of Columbia have Living Will legislation. Even though we could not get enabling legislation in South Dakota at that time, I decided that it didn't matter. I decided that it was a personal matter between patient and physician. If Lee Marvin could be made to pay millions of dollars in palimony for alleged verbal promises, I decided that a handwritten statement from a patient should be every bit as much a binding agreement if I were to withhold treatment at a patient's request. Therefore, I began having my patients write out their wishes in their own handwriting and dating and signing the document. I then placed a copy in their clinic chart and a copy in their hospital chart. Some chose to have their attorneys draw up a legal document called the Durable Power of Attorney for Healthcare, and that was likewise placed in their charts. Even though legislation did not exist in our state at that time actually permitting the legal use of these documents, it was much better to have them in place than to have nothing at all. The most important thing that it did was to provide the families a definite course of action to follow. Young people usually have no problem talking about their own death because it is such a distant reality to most of them. This topic is seldom addressed in families of older people who are facing death, because it is uncomfortable, and people think that it is in poor taste to talk about death to someone who is close to dying. Therefore, the families are left to grope for the right course when that time comes.

I felt that these documents would be of use even if they were not recognized by statute, because documented verbal agreements are enforceable and most written agreements are enforceable, even if no attorneys are involved in their preparation.

One reason I felt compelled to have these documents in the charts stemmed from a case in California in which two physicians were prosecuted for murder a few years ago. One nurse, unable to accept the family's written statement and the family's and doctors' decision to terminate life support, went to the District Attorney's office with her disgruntlement. An attorney in that office—in my opinion, hot for political exposure—charged the doctors with murder. Now mind you, this was not a civil case of a family suing for malpractice. This was a criminal case brought by the state against the doctors. The state thought it knew better than the family or the physicians what was "right" for this 54-year-old male who had made his wishes well known to his family before his surgery.

Now I ask you, who was playing God?

The doctors were eventually acquitted, but not until tens of thousands of dollars of taxpayers' money was wasted, and not until the doctors were dragged through two years of hell and had to question everything for which they stood.

Extenuating circumstances surrounding the patient's cardio-respiratory arrest and subsequent brain death in the recovery room should have been handled in a malpractice suit at the wife's discretion, but a malpractice accusation is a far cry from a charge of murder!

For many years, we in the medical profession have been held to a strict code of "informed consent," and if we do not have informed consent, we can be sued for malpractice. The courts have upheld this time and again. Where, then, did the courts ever derive the idea that a patient could not refuse terminal life care? If patients have the right to refuse a medication or an operation when they are competent and salvageable, how can the courts logically argue that patients do not have the right to refuse in advance a treatment that may prolong their life when they are no longer competent and no longer salvageable?

Let's take a look now at these two documents and see which states allow their use.

The Living Will

The Living Will is a personal statement, often done in your own handwriting, spelling out your wishes for terminal care (1) if you are incapacitated and cannot make a competent decision and (2) if you have a terminal condition. No one can enact your Living Will unless both conditions exist. The Living Will statement should be very specific. Most Living Wills simply state that in the event of a terminal condition with no reasonable hope of recovery the patient does not want CPR (Cardiopulmonary Resuscitation). A Living Will needs to be more specific and needs to go much further than this if you want to protect yourself from artificial feedings and artificial hydration, as I do. This document should be reviewed with your doctor or doctors, and if they are not comfortable with it, it should be rewritten so that they are. More important, if your physician still does not agree with your right to self-determination, either solve the impasse with dialogue, or find another physician. An example of a handwritten living will would be as follows:

- - - - - -

If I am in a terminal condition, or my brain is not functioning to the point where I am no longer competent or able to think and act for myself and there is no reasonable hope for my recovery, I request that no artificial means of resuscitation or life-sustaining care be given. I specifically do not want CPR, antibiotics or other life-saving drugs, IV feedings, IV fluids, tube feedings or fluids via tubes into my intestines, nor do I want hand feedings or fluids by hand if I cannot feed myself, to be used to prolong my life. I believe that such procedures would not really prolong my life but only prolong my dying. I choose to die quickly and with dignity. I do request that comfort measures and pain medicines be used to ensure my comfort and dignity. I release my doctors from any and all responsibility that they could possibly be accused of undertaking by following my request.

_____   _____
Date   Signature

_____   _____
Date   Witness

_____   _____
Date   Witness

A longer and more formal Living Will has been appearing recently, drawn up in legal offices and having a more official appearance. Some people might give that document more weight because it is typed and has a legal appearance, but in my own opinion a hand-written document is hard to beat for authority and authenticity. I have seen legal documents 'signed' by totally incompetent people, the pen placed in their hand by a family member and their memory jogged to perform a memorized task. If the entire Living Will is in your handwriting, however, you had to be competent to perform that complex task.

The following is just such an example of a Living Will drawn up by attorneys, but I have altered a few of the statements into plain English to make them less confusing.

LIVING WILL DECLARATION

This document directs the medical treatment you are to receive in the event you are unable to participate in your own medical decisions and you are in a terminal condition. This document states what kind of treatment you want or do not want to receive.

This document can control whether you live or die. Prepare this document carefully. If you use this form, read it completely. You may want to seek professional help to make sure the form does what you intend and is completed without mistake. You should discuss this form and its implication with your primary physician, and you should be sure he or she explains exactly what it means and whether or not he or she will abide by your decisions. If your physician cannot abide by this document, it is meaningless.

This document will remain valid and in effect until and unless you revoke it. Review this document periodically to make sure it continues to reflect your wishes. You may amend or revoke this document at any time by notifying your physician and other healthcare providers. You should give copies of this document to your physician and your family. This form is entirely optional. If you choose to use this form, please note that the form provides signature lines for you, the two witnesses whom you have selected and a notary public.

TO MY FAMILY PHYSICIANS AND ALL THOSE CONCERNED WITH MY CARE:

I, _____, willfully and voluntarily make this declaration as a directive to be followed if I am in a terminal condition, coma, or near coma, and become unable to participate in decisions regarding my medical care.

With respect to any life-sustaining treatment, I direct the following:

(Initial only the directives you desire. If you do not agree with any of the following directives, space is provided below for you to write your own directives.)

_____ NO LIFE-SUSTAINING TREATMENT. I direct that no life-saving treatment be provided. If life-sustaining treatment is begun, terminate it.

_____ TREATMENT FOR RESTORATION. Provide life-sustaining treatment only if and for so long as you believe treatment offers a reasonable possibility of restoring to me the ability to think and act for myself.

_____ MAXIMUM TREATMENT. Preserve my life as long as possible, but do not provide treatment that is not in accordance with accepted medical standards then in effect.

_____ I wish food and water to be given by artificial means such as a tube in my nose, mouth, or intestines.

_____ I DO NOT wish food and water to be given by artificial means such as a tube in my nose, mouth or intestines if there is no hope of recovery.

___ I REFUSE FEEDINGS ADMINISTERED BY OTHER INDIVIDUALS if I am unable to feed myself and there is no hope of my recovery.

___ I REFUSE WATER AND ALL OTHER HYDRATION if I am unable to drink for myself and there is no hope of my recovery.

(If you do not agree with any of the printed directives and want to write your own, or if you want to write directives in addition to the printed provisions, or if you want to express some of your other thoughts, you can do so here or on the back of this page.)

_____

_____

_____

_____

_____

_____

_____   _____

Date   Signature

_____   _____

Address   Type or Print Name

The declarant voluntarily signed this document in my presence.

_____   _____

Witness   Address

_____   _____

Witness   Address

STATE OF _____:

COUNTY OF _____:

On this the ___ day of _____, 19___, the declarant, _____, and witnesses _____ and _____ personally appeared before the undersigned officer and signed the forgoing instrument in my presence. Dated this ___ day of _____, 19___.

_____
Notary Public

Durable Power Of Attorney For Healthcare

The Durable Power of Attorney for Healthcare is a longer, more formal, and legally more enforceable document in those states that have legislation authorizing its use. The key difference is that whereas the Living Will is a personal document between the patient and the provider, the Durable Power of Attorney for Healthcare designates a certain person to act in the patient's behalf when the patient is no longer able to do so. The designated person is called the attorney-in-fact, but that term may be misleading because that individual need not be an attorney. Usually the attorney-in-fact is a family member or close friend. Your Durable Power of Attorney for Healthcare becomes operable only when you become unable to make your own decisions, whether due to physical reasons such as coma or near-coma, or mental reasons such as dementia (memory loss or mental deterioration.) This document is more flexible than the Living Will in most respects because the Durable Power of Attorney designee has been authorized by the grantor (the patient) to make decisions for him based on his prior wishes, and these decisions can be discussed with the doctor and adapted to a particular situation.

For example, let us postulate that you had declined all treatment but you also had requested in your Durable Power of Attorney that comfort measures and pain medications be used. Then you fall and break your hip. Is treatment such as pinning of the hip declined because you wanted no treatment? If the doctor explained to your attorney-in-fact that it would be a relatively simple matter to fix the break and that it would be much more comfortable to have the break stabilized rather than the bones grinding together and causing pain, the attorney-in-fact could authorize the repair, since it is not a life-prolonging maneuver and may well be a comfort measure. However, if the situation was that of an imminent heart attack requiring open heart surgery, the attorney-in-fact could and should decline, because that is obviously a life-sustaining operation. A Durable Power of Attorney document spells out each condition separately, so that there is no question as to what the patient's wishes are. As I said, it is a much longer document, but definitely a more thorough document. If both documents exist, the Durable Power of Attorney for Healthcare legally prevails, unless the Living Will has a later enactment date. The reason I encourage the use of both is that the Living Will spells out, in the patient's own words, what his or her wishes are and serves as a beacon or guideline for the person who has been designated as the attorney-in-fact. That person can then use the flavor of the Living Will, along with personal knowledge of the patient's wishes and the strength of those wishes, to help make the judgments necessary.

The following is a basic, widely accepted form of a Durable Power of Attorney for Healthcare. The basic document and format were approved by the South Dakota Bar Association, so it should be acceptable in most states. It is used here with their kind permission. I have altered it somewhat, however, because some passages were couched in legal phrases, and I have simplified these to simple English.

DURABLE POWER OF ATTORNEY FOR HEALTHCARE

1.   DESIGNATION OF HEALTHCARE AGENT.

I, _____(Principal), hereby appoint:

_____

(Agent's name)

_____

(Address)

_____

(City, State, Zip)

_____   _____

Home Telephone   Work Telephone

as my Agent to make health and personal care decisions for me as authorized in this document.

2.   EFFECTIVE DATE AND DURABILITY.

By this document I intend to create a Durable Power of Attorney effective upon, and only during any period of incapacity in which, in the opinion of my Agent and attending physician, I am unable to make or communicate a choice regarding a particular healthcare decision.

3. AGENT'S POWERS.

I grant to my Agent full authority to make decisions for me regarding my healthcare. In exercising this authority, my Agent shall follow my desires as stated in this document or otherwise known to my Agent. In making any decision, my Agent shall attempt to discuss the proposed decision with me to determine my desires if I am able to communicate in any way. If my Agent cannot determine the choice I would want made, then my Agent shall make a choice for me based upon what my Agent believes to be in my best interests. My Agent's authority to interpret my desires is intended to be as broad as possible, except any limitations I may state below. Accordingly, unless specifically limited by Section 4, below, my Agent is authorized as follows:

A. To consent, refuse, or withdraw consent to any and all types of medical care, treatment, surgical procedures, diagnostic procedures, medication and the use of mechanical or other procedures that affect any bodily function, including (but not limited to) artificial respiration, nutritional support and hydration, and cardio-pulmonary resuscitation;

B. To have access to medical records and information to the same extent that I am entitled to, including the right to disclose the contents to others;

C. To authorize my admission to or discharge (even against medical advice) from any hospital, nursing home, residential care, assisted living or similar facility or service;

D. To contract on my behalf for any healthcare-related service or facility without my Agent's incurring personal financial liability for such contract;

E. To hire and fire medical, social service, and other support personnel responsible for my care;

F. To authorize or refuse to authorize any medication or procedure intended to relieve pain, even though such use may lead to physical damage, addiction, or hasten the moment of (but not intentionally cause) my death;

G. To make anatomical gifts of part or all of my body for medical purposes, authorize an autopsy, and direct the disposition of my remains, to the extent permitted by law;

H. To take any other action necessary to do what I authorize here, including (but not limited to), granting any waiver or release from liability required by any hospital, physician, or other healthcare provider; signing any documents relating to refusals of treatment or the leaving of a facility against medical advice, and pursuing any legal action in my name, and at the expense of my estate to force compliance with my wishes as determined by my Agent, or to seek actual or punitive damages for the failure to comply.

4. STATEMENT OF DESIRES, SPECIAL PROVISIONS, AND LIMITATIONS.

A. The powers granted above do not include the following powers or are subject to the following rules or limitations:

_____

_____

_____

B. With respect to any Life-Sustaining treatment, I direct the following:

(Initial the paragraph or paragraphs that apply.)

___ REFERENCE TO LIVING WILL. I specifically direct my Agent to follow any healthcare declaration or "Living Will" executed by me.

___ GRANT OF DISCRETION TO AGENT. I do not want my life to be prolonged, nor do I want life-sustaining treatment to be provided or continued if my Agent believes the burdens of the treatment outweigh the expected benefits. I want my Agent to consider the relief of suffering, the expense involved, and the quality as well as the possible extension of my life in making decisions concerning life-sustaining treatment.

___ DIRECTIVE TO WITHHOLD OR WITH-DRAW TREATMENT. I do not want my life to be prolonged, and I do not want life-sustaining treatment IF:

1. I have a condition that is incurable or irreversible and, without the administration of life-sustaining treatment, expected to result in death without any reasonable hope for recovery; or

2. I am in a coma or persistent vegetative state which is reasonably concluded to be irreversible.

___ DIRECTIVE FOR MAXIMUM TREAT-MENT. I want my life to be prolonged to the greatest extent possible without regard to my condition, the chances I have for recovery, or the cost of the procedures.

___ DIRECTIVE IN MY OWN WORDS:

_____

_____

_____

_____

C. WITH RESPECT TO NUTRITION AND HYDRATION, I direct the following:

(If you initial the first paragraph, do NOT initial any others.)

___ I wish food and water to be given by artificial means such as a tube in my nose, mouth, or intestines.

___ I DO NOT wish food and water to be given by artificial means such as a tube in my nose, mouth, or intestines.

___ I REFUSE feedings administered by other individuals if I am unable to feed myself and there is no hope of my recovery.

___ I REFUSE water and all other hydration if I am unable to drink for myself and there is no hope of my recovery.

5. SUCCESSORS.

If any Agent named by me shall die, become

legally disabled, resign, refuse to act, be unavailable, or be legally separated or divorced from me, I name the following (each to act alone and successively, in the order named) as successors to my Agent:

A. First Alternate Agent: _____

Address: _____

Telephone: _____

B. Second Alternate Agent: _____

Address: _____

Telephone: _____

6. PROTECTION OF THIRD PARTIES WHO RELY ON MY AGENT.

No person who relies in good faith upon my representations by my Agent or Successor Agent shall be liable to me, my estate, my heirs or assigns, for recognizing the Agent's authority.

7. NOMINATION OF GUARDIAN.

If a guardian of my person should for any reason be appointed, I nominate my Agent (or his or her successor), named above.

8. ADMINISTRATIVE PROVISIONS.

A. I revoke any prior Power of Attorney for Healthcare.

B. This Power of Attorney is intended to be valid in any jurisdiction in which it is presented.

C. My Agent shall not be entitled to compensation for services performed under this Power of Attorney, but he or she shall be entitled to reimbursement for all reasonable expenses incurred as a result of carrying out any provision of this Power of Attorney.

D. The powers delegated under this Power of Attorney are separable, so that the invalidity of one or more powers shall not affect any others.

BY SIGNING HERE, I INDICATE THAT I UNDERSTAND THE CONTENTS OF THIS DOCUMENT AND THE EFFECT OF THIS GRANT OF POWERS TO MY AGENT.

I sign my name to this Durable Power of Attorney for Healthcare on this ___ day of _____, 19___.

Signature: _____

Printed Name: _____

My current home address is:

_____

_____

_____

WITNESS STATEMENT

I declare that the person who signed or acknowledged this document is personally known to me, that he/she signed or acknowledged this Durable Power of Attorney in my presence, and that he/she appears to be of sound mind and under no duress, fraud, or undue influence. I am not the person appointed as Agent by this document, nor am I the patient's healthcare provider or an employee of the patient's healthcare provider.

Witness No. 1

_____	_____
Date	Signature
_____	_____
Telephone	Print Name
	_____
	Residence Address
	_____
	City, State, Zip

Witness No. 2

_____	_____
Date	Signature
_____	_____
Telephone	Print Name
	_____
	Residence Address
	_____
	City, State, Zip

STATE OF _____)
)SS
COUNTY OF _____)

On this the ___ day of _____,
19___, before me,_____,
the undersigned officer, personally appeared
_____, known to me
or satisfactorily proven to be the person whose
name is subscribed to the above instrument and
acknowledged that he/she executed the same
for the purposes therein contained.

In witness whereof I have hereunto set my
hand and official seal.

Notary Public

_____

(SEAL)
My commission expires:

_____

Date: _____

Changes:

A few years ago, many states did not have legislation authorizing Living Wills and Durable Powers of Attorney for Healthcare. This is changing rapidly, and the list of states without this legislation is quite small, thanks in part to the **Omnibus Reconciliation Act of 1990**. The status of these is summarized in the National Survey of State Laws, First Edition, Richard A. Leiter, Ed., 1992, pages 313-331/338-354. At this writing, it appears that Massachusetts, Michigan, New York, and possibly Pennsylvania, do not recognize Living Wills. They do, however, recognize Durable Power of Attorney for Healthcare documents.

Only Alabama, and possibly Maryland, have no statutory provisions for the Durable Power of Attorney for Healthcare. Alaska's law allows consent for treatment but not for withdrawal of treatment. These states do recognize Living Wills.

In reviewing Richard A. Leiter's tables, you will notice that many states do not allow withholding of hydration and nutrition in Living Wills. These states are Indiana, Kentucky, Maryland, Minnesota (if patient accepts it), Missouri, Nebraska, North Dakota, South Dakota, Utah and Wisconsin. States that do not allow withholding of hydration and nutrition in the Durable Power of Attorney for Healthcare laws include Minnesota, Missouri, Nebraska (unless declarant specifically gives authority), Oklahoma, Pennsylvania, South Dakota (oral), Utah, and Wisconsin (oral).

Notice that some of these states have overlap; what one doesn't cover, the other does.

Therefore, if both of these documents exist, there should be no difficulty ensuring that your wishes are carried out. However, be sure that if they are done at different times, they are compatible. In the event that you should wish to change your Durable Power of Attorney, it might be a good idea to have a section at the end for changing and updating it temporarily. However, a new document should be prepared at your earliest convenience to allay any doubts that those changes may create. Be sure to have any changes witnessed, of course. I believe that a person should review, sign and date this document periodically, because that is ongoing evidence that you really meant what you initially wrote, that you were not being pressured by anyone at one moment in time, and that your decision has been repeatedly thought about. If there ever was a question about challenging your directives, most courts would look at that ongoing review as proof of your resolve.

You should take care of this important matter soon, while it is fresh in your mind and you are able to spare your family the pain that putting it off might engender. It does not matter how young you are; it needs to be done. I also encourage you to do it even if your state is not one that allows Living Wills or Durable Power of Attorney for Healthcare. They probably will allow them soon, because the **Omnibus Reconciliation Act of 1990** contains the **Patient Self-Determination Act of 1990**, which finally declares in a legal, national forum what I have been saying all along—the patient has the right to self-determination and can choose or refuse medical care. The legal precedents have been there for years. If we treat a patient without his or her informed consent, we can be found guilty of malpractice. Where did the government ever get the idea that the patient could not refuse treatment at the end? Where did the government ever acquire the power to override a competent person's personal wishes for the care of his or her body? The decision was never the government's to make in the first place. We **are** the government. Therefore, I contend that if your state does not recognize the legality of a Living Will or Durable Power of Attorney for Healthcare, you should prepare them just the same, because your doctor (if you have a good dialogue) will probably honor them. At the least it will give the doctor and the family a guideline as to what you would have wanted when difficult decisions need to be made under duress. Most doctors want to do the right thing. Only you can let them know what that means to you when the end is near.

And when that end is near and you have done nothing, what then? If neither a Living Will nor a Durable Power of Attorney for Healthcare exists, you will be cared for in the traditional manner, like Theresa, who lived in our nursing home for so, so long.

● ● ●

Before her stroke Theresa was the picture of life— aggressive, bold, decisive, fun-loving, and with a sense of humor that wouldn't quit. After her stroke, she couldn't walk, talk or use her right side. Her husband had preceded her in death, and there being no one to care for her at home, she had no place else to go but to a nursing home.

At first she could feed herself—somewhat, at least—with her left hand, but her whole being was changed. She was not the same person. There was no life in those once shining eyes, only confusion; there was no life in that voice either, just gibberish. Then after the second and third strokes, nothing—no recognition, no opening of the eyes, no voice, no movement that was purposeful. She had become what we have come to know in our everyday language as a "vegetable"—not a kind term for a human being, perhaps, but it remains in our vocabulary because it is so descriptive. It describes a living organism that has respiration, intake of nutrients and elimination of waste, and nothing more! There are not even recognizable thought processes that make it at least "animal." The term remains "vegetable," because even an animal can move, react and respond to its environment, withdraw from pain, and think enough to learn how to find food and shelter. The term "vegetable" describes all that has been lost in one word. And in functional terms that was what poor Theresa had become. She could do absolutely nothing for herself, not even scratch her nose if it itched. And she probably couldn't comprehend that it itched in the first place.

She could feel pain, however, because before she was totally immobile, she somehow got loose of her protective restraints and fell to the floor, fracturing her hip. She could moan in pain, but could do nothing about it.

Now here we had basically the opposite case from David's. Indeed it was Theresa and so many like her that led me to the path that I eventually took with David's care, because I can't just think about the "what" of patient care; I am cursed to always ponder the "why" as well.

Theresa's case was opposite David's, in that here the family made the decision early to do nothing, not to put her through any operations or any other procedure, sure that her death was nigh at hand. We gave her Morphine and kept her clean and did all the usual day-to-day things we do, but Theresa was blessed with a heart strong enough for three people, and so it beat and it beat and it beat. It beat for nearly five more years. And although the family decided to do "nothing," they never even thought about food and water. That was a given. So we continued to feed and hydrate her.

Her fractured left hip, which had never been repaired, contracted up, up, and over her right thigh, so that it was nearly in her chest. And it seemed to many that it got more painful for her as it did so. She could not be rolled from side to side very well, because of the abnormal configuration of her hips and legs; therefore she developed bed sores, decubitus ulcers, that, because of the constant pressure, never healed and undoubtedly caused her more discomfort.

Her arms and hands likewise contracted, and by that time it was painful for her to have her extremities pried apart for a bath. And she needed that bath greatly, because she had developed a continuous foul odor from constant urine dribbling and stooling. But worst of all was the vaginal odor. Since her legs contracted tightly across one another and because she was seldom upright, the vaginal mucous could not drain naturally, and like any fluid that becomes stagnant in nature, it became infected. And as it trickled slowly onto her skin, it irritated everything it touched. The smell became so noticeable that you could smell it in the hallway, and there were days when it could nauseate you when you entered the room.

The daily routine then was to have two aids pry apart her legs as hard as they dared, while a nurse douched the vagina and let the soap and pus and water drain out onto the protective pads with the urine and stool. Then came the plunger full of vaginal antibiotic cream. Then they stripped the bedding. By then it was lunch time—time to "poke it in and dig it out" again.

This was life for Theresa. It got so depressing, as it usually does for about three-quarters of a million people a year, that her family could no longer come to visit her except on a rare occasion. I am not in any way demeaning the family. It was not their fault. They couldn't handle the hopelessness. In fact, their visits reminded me of people going to the cemetery to pay their respects to a departed loved one. There was absolutely nothing they could say; perhaps they could stroke her forehead and hope that she was comforted by it, but the overwhelming sentiment by that point in time was, and I quote, "Why can't the poor thing just die."

But she couldn't die because she had never made any plans on how to handle this situation.

And the family, while refusing "treatments," never considered spoon feedings and syringes full of water as "treatments." In fact, our staff never considered them as anything but the natural thing to do either, since it was what they had always done. So while the family was paying their last respects and wishing she could die, we continued to care for Theresa, keeping her alive. And it still haunts me. Dozens of Theresas haunt me, because I know now that I did them no service. Disservice would be a more apt term. I should have let go sooner, but I didn't know. It takes time and experience to mature into these things. And I certainly got no training in this matter. The entire medical community is poleaxed when it comes to this issue. How can the professors teach the students when the professors haven't faced the issue? So Theresa went on living her death year after year, and you may do the same if you fail to act.

5

SPECIFIC CASES AND LEGAL PRECEDENTS

Having allowed the families of several terminal patients access to this manuscript during the pre-publication phase, it has become apparent to me that although they have become more conversant with the principles involved and more comfortable with the decisions they had been leaning toward, they still needed individual assurances that these principles applied to their particular cases. Therefore, I have added this section to attempt to address specific questions that may arise in readers' minds.

I have thought long and hard about the questions involved in this decision-making process, and my own conclusions have been written in the other chapters. As I did further reading of legal cases to put together this chapter, it was very gratifying to know that there has been recent case law that substantiates exactly what I have been proposing for the last several years. The major point that I have made and stressed is that the choice of refusing all modalities of treatment, including food and hydration, is a choice that is every person's right to make based upon their constitutional right of freedom of choice. I have told these families that this is what I would do for myself or my own family member, and this has personalized my advice to them and made it easier for them to apply to their own case. I would not offer a plan of action that I have not already accepted for either myself or my family. To compile this chapter I had originally thought to give several theoretical scenarios to show people how these theories might apply to different cases. However, I found several actual court cases to strengthen the validity of my proposals. Before relating those, however, let me offer some of my actual patients as examples of what can be done to avoid unwanted cares.

• • •

Ellen is a 47-year-old Registered Nurse who is also a close personal friend. We have had long talks about the principles involved herein, and she understands their implications completely, having worked in a nursing home for many years. Recently she was found to have abnormalities of her thyroid function, and a thyroid scan revealed cancer of the thyroid gland. A few days before surgery she sat down and wrote a Living Will and a Durable Power of Attorney for Healthcare based on the examples given in this book. She had read the manuscript, and she wanted to make it very clear to her family what her wishes were if her surgical outcome was poor. Most important, being involved in long-term care for many years herself, she wanted to "spare my husband and children the emotional and physical burdens of making these decisions." She also wanted to "spare them the financial burden long-term care would have caused." Ellen knew what it was like keeping brain-dead people alive by tube and spoon feedings and "absolutely" did not wish to be kept alive if she could not lift that spoon herself. Her Living Will and Durable Power of Attorney specifically declined CPR, surgery, feeding or hydration by IV or tube feedings if there was no reasonable hope of recovery. But her directives also spelled out that if she could not feed herself and there was no reasonable hope of her doing so in the future, no one else was to give her food and water by any external means, including spoon feedings. Ellen had cared for David in his last year of life and was, like the family, relieved for him when his suffering ordeal was over. She wanted no part of that kind of existence for herself. We were thankful that her surgery went well and these documents were not needed, but she is glad that she has them taken care of and that they are in her permanent medical record.

• • •

Mildred is an intelligent and active lady who, at 87, looks and acts more like 67. While she was being evaluated for abdominal pain, an ultrasound of the abdomen showed an aneurysm, or ballooning of the aorta, next to the right kidney artery. I have discussed with her the surgery for this condition, as well as possible complications, such as anesthesia reactions, infections, prolonged hospitalization, and even the possibility of death. I have made it very clear to her that the aneurysm could rupture if it is not fixed, and if it does so she could bleed to death in a matter of minutes. She chose "not to have surgery at my age." She knows that at age 87 she will not live very much longer and that bleeding to death very quickly is, in her words, "one way to go." This sounds to her like a basically painless way to die. Additionally, Mildred has chosen no intervention "in case of a terminal event of any type." She wishes to refuse food and water to hasten the end of her dying if she is unable to feed herself. She is facing and accepting "the inevitability of death." It is my experience that this acceptance of death is typical of the octogenarian in general.

●　　●　　●

Don is a 50-year-old attorney and close personal friend who does a majority of his legal work in estate planning. He has known for years that Living Wills and Powers of Attorney are important matters, but after reading this manuscript he admitted that he had not thought about the food and water issue, not really realizing what so many people go through in the nursing home. He had not really thought about food and water as part of the choices to be made, thinking more about the classical medical treatments. He confided that after reading this manuscript, he and his wife changed their documents to specifically refuse spoon feedings and hydration if they cannot do them themselves. In addition, he had his two law partners read the manuscript. Neither of them had thought the issue through to that end, because they have not been involved in the day-to-day care of slowly dying patients.

It is important, then, to point out that three intelligent, informed and competent attorneys, who have been very active in estate law and estate planning, did not have the background to fully "advise" their clients in this very critical matter. It is equally important to point out that if you fail to put your wishes in writing, you will be at the mercy of a legal system that does not take care of dying patients. It is the same legal system that in Massachusetts took nineteen months to affirm the right of Joseph Saikewicz to refuse chemotherapy, fourteen months after he was dead!

Until the past few years, it has been relatively rare for patients to have their wishes written down. In the past it was debatable whether or not putting your wishes into writing would have been honored by a court of law.   Many, if not most, in the medical field feel that the courts have over-stepped their bounds by taking the decision out of patients' and families' hands in certain cases. In the case of a lifelong incompetent person, courts have tended to treat the patient like a child and protect him or her at all cost. In the case of Joseph Saikewicz, a 67-year-old severely retarded man who developed leukemia, the court very slowly, though eventually, concluded that since the effect of chemotherapy on his type of leukemia was very poor, and since he could not understand why he needed needles and IVs, and since he therefore would not hold still and would require restraints, and since the side effects of chemotherapy would produce pain and sickness, it was deemed reasonable for his guardian to refuse treatment. Forcing the patient in this case to take chemotherapy went beyond normal, ordinary care.

The "reasonable person" doctrine, or what a reasonable person would do in a given case, has been used as a precedent in U.S. law time and again, and not just in the area of healthcare. For instance, if a person claims that what he did in a given situation was all that he could have done in that situation, courts have analyzed that particular situation and attempted to decide what a reasonable person would have done. The situation that I like to present to students is, "Should a person ever let another person drown?" On the surface it would appear that a quick, "No," would suffice. If you had a life raft and someone were drowning and you purposefully rowed away from them, the courts might say that doing so could be construed as manslaughter. But what if your life raft had eighteen nonswimmers in it, was only built for ten, and was in imminent danger of sinking? The court would find that a reasonable person might be forced to let one person drown to save the other eighteen.

Case law has been written that supports this theory in terminal care as far back as 1977. In Lane vs. Candura, Mrs. Candura was a 77-year-old widow who had developed gangrene and needed her foot and leg amputated to prevent infection from taking her life. She refused, and her daughter, Mrs. Lane, appealed for guardianship. Mrs. Lane was granted guardianship based on testimony by a psychiatrist that her mother was incompetent. This case is important because the psychiatrist and the lower court used circular reasoning to conclude incompetence. Although relatively lucid and competent in most ways, they charged that she was incompetent because she accepted certain death over surgery. Since no competent person would want to die (in their opinion), any person making the choice of dying had to be incompetent. Since Mrs. Candura made this choice, she therefore had to be incompetent. Their argument was based on an assumption that guaranteed their conclusion! It was like saying, "All apples are red. This fruit looks like an apple and tastes like an apple but it is green. Since all apples are red this cannot be an apple." If you start your argument with a conclusion and use that conclusion to prove your argument, you are guilty of circular reasoning. Fortunately the Massachusetts Appeals Court system determined that Mrs. Candura was competent in most things, and the basis for her refusal of care was that she did not want to be a burden to her family, that she did not believe that surgery would cure her problem, that she had been very unhappy with life since her husband had passed away, and that she had no desire to extend her life. The Court therefore determined that her decision was based on reasonable logic. Further, since one of the major tenets of constitutional law in America is that of personal freedom, **the court ruled that a competent person has the personal freedom to refuse medical treatments, even if that refusal is likely to result in his or her death.**

The competent patient is one matter, the

previously competent patient who is rendered incompetent is another. The most famous is the Karen Quinlan case, but it was basically limited to discontinuation of a respirator for a person not yet "brain dead." Karen was in a persistent vegetative state but still had some basic reflex activity, so she did not meet the guidelines for brain death. The lower court had denied her father's right to terminate life support based on this fact. However, New Jersey's Supreme Court cited her previous verbal statements that she would not want to be kept alive by a life-support system as the declarations of a reasonable person and cited her ultimate "right to privacy," which could be sought by her father on her behalf. Since there was overwhelming evidence that she had no reasonable hope of recovery, the state Supreme Court ruled that the family and the treating physician could make the ultimate decision as to whether she would accept or refuse a medical treatment. In this particular case they did ask that the family first consult with the ethics committee before proceeding. This affirmed the individual's right to self-determination and set the stage for the **Self-Determination Act of 1990** and the Elizabeth Bouviae case.

We now have progressed from incompetent from birth through formerly competent but rendered incompetent due to severe brain damage; we now arrive at the brain-competent patient, Elizabeth Bouviae. Elizabeth was a 28-year-old female who had suffered from cerebral palsy since birth. She had slowly deteriorated over 28 years to be quadriplegic, bedridden, and almost totally paralyzed except for some movement in a few of her fingers and some head and facial movements. Because of severe arthritis she was in constant pain and, therefore, a morphine pump was being used to automatically inject the pain killer morphine sulfate through a tube under her skin for temporary, but only partial, pain relief. She was alert and competent, and elected to terminate her suffering by refusing further food and water. A lower court denied her this right, but the appeals court reversed the lower court, stating that the tubes in her chest and stomach were "the forced intrusion of an artificial mechanism into her body against her will." The higher court cited her right to privacy and her right to self-determination. Additionally, one of the judges in a separate opinion went on to say, "I believe she has an absolute right to effectuate that decision. This state and the medical profession, instead of frustrating her desire, should be attempting to relieve her suffering by permitting and, in fact, assisting her to die with ease and dignity. The fact that she is forced to suffer the ordeal of self-starvation to achieve her objective is in itself inhumane." This judge went on to say, "If there is ever a time when we ought to be able to get the government off our backs, it is as we face death."

This author finds it incredible that a terminally ill patient in severe pain may be denied the right to die quickly, depending on the whim or personal bias of a judge or prosecutor or doctor, while any healthy person can buy a gun or drive a car into a bridge abutment at 100 mph. We cannot stop suicide in healthy people; but the very people who are too ill to help themselves, we force to go on with their painful, helpless, hopeless existence. It reminds me of school-yard bullies who cannot beat up on the strong, so instead they beat up on the weak.

The judge in the Bouviae case cited "self-starvation" in his opinion, and in another New Jersey case, the court allowed removal of the "feeding tube." I have seen, over and over, cases in which feeding was either terminated or was physically impossible to perform, while hydration went on and on. It has become crystal clear to me that once a decision not to pursue FULL feeding has been made, we must immediately stop both food and water, and give adequate doses of morphine sulfate by continuous infusion to be sure that we have alleviated suffering. It has become my firm conviction that hydration without feeding is slow torture. You can keep the body going for weeks on water alone. (Witness the people who exited the concentration camps in Germany and Poland in 1945.) The very act of trying to be "kind" by hydrating terminal patients transforms us into unwitting tormentors. Once the decision has been made to withdraw all but pain relief, we must immediately stop all food and water and allow the quick path of dehydration to prevail. This can be the final common pathway for the 5-year-old comatose child with brain trauma, the 50-year-old with brain cancer, or the 80-year-old with Alzheimer's Disease. It will work quickly for the 70-year-old with a massive stroke, just as it will work quickly for the 40-year-old with terminal multiple sclerosis. But it cannot be YOUR final common pathway if you do not make your wishes known now, while you are competent.

That brings me to share with you my feelings, thoughts and wishes for my final days, and my hope that I will stir at least some of you to take up pen and paper and with the stroke of that pen, relieve your family of that final burden.

6

END GAME

IN THIS DISCUSSION I HAVE SO FAR dealt with individuals whose brains have deteriorated but whose bodies continue to function. This will encompass the vast majority of people, but there is a smaller subset of people whose brains function well but whose bodies have deteriorated to the point of helplessness and hopelessness beyond the point of no return. Therefore, I would like to tell you Neal's story.

Originally I had not included Neal's story in this book because I had promised both Neal and his wife that I would keep our final conversation just between us. The more I pondered Neal's story, however, the more I felt compelled to tell it because it embodies the whole issue of choice so well. I, therefore, spoke with Neal's widow and she too feels that the telling may help someone and wishes the story to be told.

● ● ●

Neal was a 55-year-old diabetic who had suffered with "brittle" or hard to control diabetes since childhood. Over the decades he had lost feeling in his feet and developed blisters that slowly enlarged. The toes, then the feet, and eventually both lower legs were amputated in slow but systematic fashion, surgery after surgery. Next his kidneys began to shut down and he started to swell. Lastly, his fingers were not only turning numb, but getting dry gangrenous spots as well. As the gangrene spread, finger after finger was amputated. When he lost the thumb on the left hand, it rendered that hand useless, except for changing positions. Then the hand had to be amputated as well, which left him with two fingers and a thumb on the right hand and those had very little feeling left.

During this time his bladder became weak, then totally paralyzed, unable to constrict and squeeze out urine. This meant that his wife had to pass a catheter through his penis every six hours to drain it for him, since he had no hands left with which to do it.

At this stage, Neal was totally dependent on his wife, and to her everlasting credit, she stood by him through it all and did not put him in a nursing home. He was unable to do anything for himself except change the channels on the television using one finger to press buttons on the remote control, and reach for a snack that she had put on the table by the bed. The bed had long since been placed in the living room so that Neal, unable to move except to crawl around on his stumps in the bed, could get some sunlight and see something of the outdoors through the picture window.

More and more he grew weaker so that getting bathed, catheterized and fed became hard work, the type of hard work that only those who have lived through such a catastrophic illness can understand. And then his right hand started becoming gangrenous, and I made my last house call for Neal. He was very matter-of-fact when he said that he'd had enough surgery. In fact, he was not passionate about it—simply logical. His conversation went thus:

"Doc, I've had enough. I'm not going back. I know they'll want to operate. I'm not going to let them carve me up any more. If they take the rest of this hand, then I'll be **totally** helpless. I won't even be able to change the channels on the TV. That's no life."

I had to agree.

We discussed various matters for a while, then he asked, "What happens if I don't take any medicine; no insulin, or anything?" I responded that his sugar would continue to climb and eventually he would go into a coma and die.

Less than two weeks later, Neal was dead. What did he do? What did he decide? Whose right is it to decide? Certainly not the state—they don't have to live in his body, with his misery and his pain. Certainly not me—I don't know enough to make the right decision for someone else. Could you decide for Neal? No. You can decide for you, and only you!

● ● ●

In this dialogue I have tried to show you what life is like for many brain damaged, terminally ill patients. Most people think of "terminal" as meaning that death is imminent. That is only an interpretation based on time. The people I am talking about are terminal in the same sense that their life is coming to an end and the process is not reversible, though it may take them years to come to that end. In my opinion, however, it is just as terminal as metastatic cancer, because it will eventually kill them. It just does so much more slowly.

Ask any soldier who has seen the horrors of war, and he will tell you that he would rather be shot outright than tortured slowly. In this battlefield, I will take lung cancer over Alzheimer's Disease any day. The slow, killing dementia that we are talking about here has multiple original causes but one end result. It kills you just as surely as cancer, but it is so much more degrading because it first robs you of the very essence of human existence. It takes your memories, then your personality, then your ability to care for your own hygiene, then your ability to enjoy any activities active or passive, then finally even the ability to eat. We caregivers can do nothing about the first four things, but we can "poke it in and dig it out." Institutions even begin to pride themselves on how well someone is doing based on how regularly their bowels evacuate and how low their enema list is from day to day. This is progress?

During medical school and internship, we routinely received patients with massive brain damage from strokes or head trauma. Our team would be reviewing the case when invariably someone would ask, "What can we do?" In response, a common refrain (spoken but never written) was, "Close the door." This implied that we could do nothing; therefore, we should close the door and let them die in peace. But we were trained to treat, and treat we did. No one wanted to face the greater question.

I cannot speak for anyone else; I can speak only for myself. It is my opinion that dying of dehydration is an easier and more dignified death than being force fed for years and dying slowly of multiple system shutdown and general malnutrition. The coma that ensues within several days of dehydration protects us from the pain. In contradistinction, lying in bed for five—possibly ten—years, as Tom has, is far more painful than death in a few days due to dehydration. His rectal sores, groin rashes and decubitus ulcers on his hips make it impossible for him to find a comfortable position. When we are talking about humane caregiving, there is only one choice for me. Death due to refusal to be fed and watered and subsequent dehydration is quick and humane.

It is my further opinion that this is the last thing I can do for society as a whole and my family in particular. I can refuse to be a burden upon my family and further refuse to be a burden on society, hoping to set an example for others to do the same. By so doing, we could free up billions of dollars that could be then appropriated to assure virtually every child in America food, shelter and education. Only when we accomplish this will we truly "choose life."

I will not speak for anyone else. I can only end by giving my opinion based upon years of firsthand experience in caring for the dying demented and telling you what I want for myself. Additionally, from my hundreds of patient-physician conversations, I can extrapolate from what seems to be nearly 100% agreement in our midwest community to what I believe to be a nationwide sentiment, and that is that people want to die quickly when their time is up. I have yet to meet a single person who wants to be kept alive or be spoon-fed when their brain is no longer functioning in any reasonable manner. However, no one seems to be able to make that decision for a third person with any type of consistency. So after I have given you my opinion and my last wishes, it remains to you to decide for yourself what you want and to take charge of this important matter now, before it is too late. Once you are considered incompetent, no one can make the decision for you, and you will be condemned to life.

I will finish, then, by telling you how I feel about my own terminal care and leave the rest up to you.

I pray that I will die quickly, with a massive stroke or heart attack, so that I never knew what hit me. Like anyone else, I want to live a long life, but only if my brain—the essence of who I am—is healthy. I dread the degradation and humiliation of lying in bed, my arms and legs contorted like Hilda's and Jessica's by contractures, unable to die. I do not want to be wandering the halls when I am 85, like Barbara, unable to find my own room. I do not want to be lying in a pool of urine and feces at 90, hollering for my parents who have been dead for 60 years. I do not want to be constantly a bother to a nursing staff by wandering out of the facility to feed my geese or to return to a home that I can never find. I do not want the humiliation of nurses not wanting to take care of me because I keep pinching their nipples or caressing their behinds when I get the chance. That is not who I am, and when who I am is gone, then let my body be gone as well.

Almost all of these patients want to be left alone. They say over and over, "I have lived a good life," "I have lived long enough," "It is just too much struggle," "I wish I could just die." That is my wish, too. One day I made the comment that these patients can't die with dignity. One nurse replied, "Hell, they can't even live with dignity." She was so sadly right.

When my brain is no longer healthy, I do not want any intervention. I do not have to be in a true coma to want this. If my memory is so poor that my activities of daily living are no longer do-able or enjoyable, I want to pass quickly and quietly away. I do not want to be a burden on my family emotionally, and I do not want to drain our life savings on a $2,000/month "existence." I want a quick, $2,000 funeral that takes a few days, not a $200,000 funeral that takes five years to get done with. I do not want resources wasted on me after there is no hope, when kids all around the globe are starving to death or have no roof over their heads. I want to be remembered as a vibrant, caring doctor who was full of life and not, "the Gomer in 109 with the bed sores." I want to be remembered as crazy Kenny, who in his will designated $2,000 for a pine box funeral and $5,000 for a party for his friends and family to see him off.

So when I cannot remember days and dates, places and names, I invoke my right to self-determination. Without question, I refuse CPR. I refuse surgery unless it is strictly to relieve a very painful condition that Morphine cannot handle. I refuse antibiotics to treat an infection such as pneumonia, which Osler so nicely called "the old man's friend." I refuse IV feedings or IV fluids to prolong my life. I refuse food supplements from some well-meaning dietitian who is trying to keep my body from wasting when my mind is already wasted.

Most importantly, when I can no longer function enough to lift my own spoon and find my mouth, when my existence is so far gone that I cannot do that one last thing necessary to survive, I refuse to be fed and watered. If I cannot feed myself, it is time to die. It is time to finish the final chapter and get out of the way—to make room for the living. This is my final responsibility to society. Let the living live!

At the end, I ask of my doctor that I be left alone. This is not the raving of a grumpy, demented old man. This is the request of a young man who has thought long and hard about these issues. So I say to my doctor, whomever that turns out to be:

Let me die in peace. I do not believe that dying of dehydration is cruel or painful. It is nature's way with all of the animal kingdom. If I cannot feed myself, do not hand-feed me or pour liquids into me. Just clean me up two

or three times a day, comb my hair, and make me look as though I have at least a little dignity left. And if my dying like this bothers anyone, then on your way out, Doctor, please close the door!

WHAT TO DO NEXT

1. Take pen and paper and make a Living Will.

A. In your own handwriting write down what you want done if you become ill and incapacitated.

B. Spell out clearly what you want done about treating or not treating infections.

C. Spell out exactly how you feel about food and hydration by tube, syringe, or spoon, if you cannot feed yourself.

D. Make it clear that you are not afraid of death, if that is your feeling, and that you believe this is the right course of action for you.

E. Request that pain medicines and comfort measures be used.

F. Release your caregivers from legal responsibility for carrying out your wishes.

Feel free to photocopy the Living Will on Page 59 and use it if you prefer.

2. See your attorney and make out a Durable Power of Attorney for Healthcare or feel free to copy the one on Page 65.

A. Fill out the appropriate blanks and sign and date it and have it witnessed.

B. Be sure that, if you do not wish to be kept alive by artificial or hand feedings and hydration, you make this clear in your Durable Power of Attorney for Healthcare.

3. Sit down with your family physician(s) and talk these things over. If they do not agree to abide by your stated desires, find a doctor who does—most will honor your wishes.

A. Give your physician(s) copies of both documents and have them placed in the front of your chart in plain sight (or they will get lost in the stack).

B. Ask that the outside folder of your chart be marked in red ink, notifying everyone that these documents exist.

C. Be sure that your hospital chart has a copy of both documents with the same instructions.

D. Give a copy of each document to your attorney and your closest family members.

E. Carry a copy of both documents whenever you are traveling.

Additional copies of
DOCTOR, PLEASE CLOSE THE DOOR
by Kenneth A. Bartholomew,
may be ordered by sending a check or
money order for $12.95 postpaid for
each copy to:

Distinctive Publishing Corp.
P.O. Box 17868
Plantation, FL 33318-7868
(305) 975-2413

Quantity discounts are also available
from the publisher.